# 'Operation Exporter':

## Britain's 1941 Battle of Syria

J P Hyde

'Operation Exporter' : Britain's 1941 Battle of Syria

ISBN-13: 978-1987439694

# DEDICATION

First, I would like to thank my professors throughout my college experience. Especially, Professor Harrison of Southern Oregon University, for his knowledge and teaching.

To my son, thank you for being who you are and constantly challenging me on a daily basis.

To my wonderful wife, you are my inspiration. Thank you for you encouragement, understanding, and help. I could not have done this without you. You are amazing.

# CONTENTS

# INTRODUCTION

When considering the Middle East there exists a colorful history. History of controversy, religion, and empires to name just a few. Over the past thousands of years, the Middle East has been a hot bed of culture, intelligence, religious starts, and a host of so much more.

Unfortunately, violence and war covered much of the region for as long as history has been written. Hittites, Amorites, Persians, or any other of numerous empires that have come and gone in the area, but Europeans against Europeans? Specifically, the battle between the British and the French.

I have chosen to address the battle of the two great European nations took place in 1941...known as Operation Exporter. This battle pitted not only the British and her allies against the French and their allies, but it also put French against French.

Many theories or conspiracies have emerged after World War 2 that knowledge of this battle and specific information was kept purposely quiet by the British. While there is not much evidence to support this claim, it is any interesting suggestion that may hold a certain amount of relevance when considering the lack of material available.

That is conspiracy I wish to dispel in these following pages. There is information available...you simply have to look. Sure, we will see there were numerous potential reasons one might wish specific details remain 'missing'.

However, most European nations since approximately 12th century, have worked tirelessly to record and document centuries of history. Woven strands of time from long ago to have now created a much fuller tapestry displaying a picture of the past.

With these improvements to record keeping, it has been increasingly difficult, whether it be an individual or entire nation to keep all events hidden. Not all facts can remain simply 'missing'.

The wins-and/or-losses between nations and people have created the landscape of our world today. Although records…the events themselves…the truth of history cannot be altered to fit any singular agenda. The good, the bad, and all that accompanied are now fact. No matter who wishes truth known or not…it still exists.

# 1: THE SETTING

The British had been attempting to get the United States to join the war for quite a period. One of the biggest selling points the British used was to free the peoples and countries that had been overrun and occupied by Nazi Germany, and since 1940, this also included France. Until France surrendered to Germany, they were Britain's biggest ally in the European theatre.

The conspiracy states that if word got out the British were waging a battle against France, after their surrender, then Britain may lose the backing of the United States, and the United States would not enter the war at all. As stated, there is not much evidence to support these claims but they are an interesting thought to make. Let us look back at some historical facts that led up to these events eliminating the gossip, speculation, and theories.

The conclusion of the First World War brought about changes throughout the world. For the Middle East, the Ottoman Empire had ruled for the past few centuries later defeated during the war by the British, French and their allies. This shift of power in the world led to the formation of the League of Nations.

The League of Nations determined that the peoples of the Middle East were not ready to govern themselves and needed oversight by other nations; these Middle Eastern nations referred to as 'mandated nations' of European countries.

Article 22 of the Covenant of the League of Nations, dated 28 June 1919 expressed the reasoning against autonomy of those nations. Article 22 states:

*"To those colonies and territories which as a consequence of the late war have ceased to be under the sovereignty of the States which*

*formerly governed them and which are inhabited by peoples not yet able to stand by themselves under the strenuous conditions of the modern world, there should be applied the principle that the well-being and development of such peoples form a sacred trust of civilization and that securities for the formance of this trust should be embodied in this Covenant.*

*The best method of giving practical effect to this principle is that tutelage of such peoples should be entrusted to advanced nations..."* (1)

This mandate took the power from these beleaguered nations and kept it in the hands of westernized European countries. Because of the new mandates set on by the League of Nations, France received the territories of Lebanon and Syria while Britain received the territories of Palestine, TransJordan, and Iraq.

Almost immediately, these western nations faced rebellions and uprisings in their mandated areas. During the First World War in an effort to win, the British, French and their backers promised people of the Middle East freedoms and a host of things if they aided the Allies in their quest of defeating the Ottoman Empire in the region. The people's response to these promises was the Allies in the eventual defeat of the Ottoman Empire.

Less than a year after the conclusion of the war, the result became apparent to the people. They traded one ruling empire for another and what they received was empty promises to all.

The people in the mandated territories realized that the European formed League of Nations believed that they were inept to be able to govern themselves. These realizations began causing disturbances for their mandated overseers to contend.

Twenty years of dealing with uprisings and rebellions in their mandated territories took a toll on France and Britain. Costing the "advanced" nations not only money, but military strength, munitions, and many other valuable resources. Unforeseen at the time things were just going to get worse for them.

When World War 2 broke out on the European mainland in 1939, Syria and Lebanon were mandated territories of France while TransJordan, Palestine, and Iraq were mandated territories of Britain as per the League of Nations after the conclusion of World War 1. (2)

The British and French not only have unruly inhabitants of their overseas territories to manage, now with the German war machine and the Nazi regime on their front step.

In July of 1939, the President of Syria, Hashim al-Atassi, and his government resigned as a protest to the Turkish government being awarded the city of Alexandretta, which had been part of Syria until this incorporation into Turkey. (3)

President Atassi's resignation came when he learned that a month previous France had signed an agreement with Turkey (Franco-Turkish Mutual Aid Agreement) in which the French stated they would be leaving Alexandretta in July. This gave the peoples living in Alexandretta the opportunity to get either Syrian or Lebanese nationality. However, six weeks prior to the onset of World War 2 Alexandretta became annexed into the Turkish Republic. This agreement and annexation by Turkey solidified Turkey's backing of Western Powers. (4)

President Atassi and his government believing that the French were not making strides to give Syria its complete independence helped lead to his resignation.

The French government reeling from this sudden government collapse responded quickly and dissolved the Syrian Chamber of Deputies, suspended the Syrian Constitution, and then placed all foreign affairs and the defense of Syria directly into French hands. Later, that leads to the creation and establishment of a pro-French government in Syria. The French also separated Syria into smaller states in hopes of better managing the area. They set up separate regimes in Jebel Druze and Latakia. (5)

In September of 1939, the French believed that Lebanon, their other mandated territory would follow the example of their neighbor. The French assumed the Lebanese government instead of resigning would go another direction and try to become completely independent of France. Before that could happen, the French proactive in their approach stepped in suspending the Lebanese constitution and took over the powers of the cabinet. (6)

France fell to German control in June of 1940 establishing the government of Vichy France. This new 'Vichy' government was a different form of government then before and loyal to Nazi Germany.

Loyalty to the Nazi regime was believed to be in an effort of self-preservation for France. Instead, they established a Franco/German collaborate.

The Vichy government was said to be autonomous and allowed to do what they wanted. However, that only held true if decisions or otherwise were made for France but served the best interest and approved by the German government.

With all new rules and regulation outlined as needed for the time…the mandated territories of France were thusly left under the helm, leadership and guidance of this newly established Vichy government.  (7)

# 2: THE MAIN PLAYERS

The British military spread thin around the globe. Constant resupplying was becoming another task in itself with the German U-boat crews wreaking havoc throughout the seas and oceans. Nonetheless, there was more to come for the British. The French mandated territories.

The British find themselves in another predicament that has to be dealt with. Not only for the immediate threat imposed, but also communications, shipping and resupplying, and for the large quantity of oil reserves in the area for the war effort. General Archibald Wavell was chosen by British government to deal with this.

General Wavell was respected and had a long successful military career with the British. Attending military school at Sandhurst where he graduated at the top of his class. A commissioned officer in the British Army in 1901. Wavell served with distinction and huge success during the Boer War. During World War 1, cost the loss of his left eye. In 1917, he served under British General Edmund Allenby during the Egyptian Campaign, he later wrote a biography of General Allenby.

In 1939, the British government tasked General Wavell with creating the Middle East Command. The main objectives of the Middle East Command were: protect the Suez Canal and its vital shipping zones and to be kept under British control, protect the oil fields throughout the Middle East to keep reserves filling, and most important keep the British and her allies' militaries moving.

Quickly after the formation of the Middle East Command General Wavell and his command were put to the test. The Italian regime sent a million soldiers into

North Africa. Their purposes...expel the British from the area and take control of the Suez Canal. Vastly outnumbered General Wavell achieved success in defending the Suez Canal against the Italian onslaught.

However, General Wavell soon found himself on the losing end of battles in North Africa when Germany in 1941 sent Field Marshall Rommel into the area and he quickly pushed the British military out of Libya.

Field Marshall Rommel was a top German commander. He had several successes in early European campaigns of World War 2. Rommel became famous for his North African campaigns. His tactics and battle strategies earned him the nickname "The Desert Fox." Rommel was skilled in his attacks against the British. He was able to repel most counter attacks launched against his armies. Rommel, highly decorated, respected by all, lost his standing with the German High Command when he was finally defeated and driven out of North Africa in 1943 by Allied forces. Before being tried and judged by his government, Rommel committed suicide at his home in Germany.

The British being pushed around in North Africa was dire for not only the British but also their allies. When the British lost Libya to the German aggression, this gave the Axis Powers a firm hold in North Africa. With the Germans established strongly in Libya it gave them, a point to constantly threaten British positions in Egypt. This German position in North Africa gave them a point in which to launch assaults against the Suez Canal and the British troops protecting it.

Wavell's recent defeats in North Africa and his tumultuous relationship with Prime Minister Churchill, General Wavell was replaced with General Auchinleck as Commander in Chief of the Middle East Command.

General Wavell was transferred to India as Commander in Chief then on to Burma to defend against the advancing Japanese military. (8) (9)

Assisting General Wavell with the task of controlling operations in Vichy controlled Syria and Lebanon was British General Henry Maitland Wilson.

General Wilson became a commissioned officer in the British military in 1900. General Wilson served the British during the Second Boer War. During World War 1, he was part of the commanding group of the 41st Division and New Zealand Division. By 1939, Wilson found himself commanding troops in Egypt then in Greece for the British.

In 1941, General Wilson was commanding troops in the British mandated territories of the Middle East. At the end of 1941, General Wilson was the Commander in Chief of the Middle East. He replaced General Auchinleck. Who had replaced General Wavell, Wilson's former commanding officer, just a few months before.

General Wilson would go on later and replace United States General Dwight Eisenhower as Supreme Allied Commander of the Mediterranean. (10)

The British would not face issues in Syria alone. Their aid came in the form of 'Free French' forces also opposing Vichy government. Leader of the Free French forces General Charles de Gaulle.

General de Gaulle had served the French military with distinction during World War 1. In the years between the wars, he was very vocal for the French needs to upgrade and modernize their defenses along their borders especially the border along Germany.

France fell to Germany in 1940 and a truce was signed. General de Gaulle refused to accept the French truce with Germany. His disagreement and strong convictions led him to London. While in London he created the 'French government in exile' or as referred to later the 'Free French'.

The Vichy government feeling threatened by General de Gaulle and Hitler also pushing for defeat, the Free French movement led by General Charles de Gaulle, was condemned to death and marked him as an enemy.

The Vichy government was established in 1940 after surrender to the conquering German military. The original French government had collapsed immediately upon surrender to Germany. The Vichy government was established in the resort town of Vichy. The Vichy government did all the dealings and negotiations with the German military and government throughout the duration of the war. The Vichy government appeared weak and timid to the world, willing to appease and accommodate the Nazi regime. France a long time enemy of Germany, the Vichy government was a representation of the exact opposite.

The Free French government established by General de Gaulle was the opposite of the Vichy government. They had no territorial rights anywhere in the world, but were recognized by all nations. They ruled from outside of France and spoke for free French people in the world, and those within the jurisdiction of the Vichy and German governments that could not speak for themselves. The Free French did not recognize the treaty with Germany. The Free French were a strong ally of Britain for the duration of the war against the Axis Powers.

For his part, de Gaulle became the focal point for the French resistance in Europe.  In 1943, General de Gaulle had unified the resistance movement everywhere.  At the conclusion of World War 2 General Charles de Gaulle was elected leader of the newly established French government, in 1945.  (11)

Helping General Charles de Gaulle with the Free French forces is French General Catroux.  General Catroux served with the French Foreign Legion in Algeria, Morocco, and Indochina.  He had also served the French government as the governor of Damascus.

Catroux found politics somewhat unfulfilling, returning to French military service and returned to command in North Africa during the 1930's.  After France surrendered to Germany the new Vichy government removed Catroux from his post on July 26, 1940.

General Catroux, being removed from his command refused to return to France, much like de Gaulle, and refuse to serve the Vichy government.  That led him to the door of General de Gaulle and aiding him in his efforts of managing the Free French forces.

For his assistance and aid, General Charles de Gaulle assigned General Catroux to represent France Libre in both Syria and Lebanon.  General Catroux was then appointed the High Commissioner of the France Libre in Syria and Lebanon by British General Henry Maitland Wilson.  (12)

Opposing the British in the Middle East is French General Henri Dentz.  General Dentz had surrendered Paris to the invading German military in June of 1940.

When the Vichy government established, General Dentz was appointed Commander of the Army of Levant or called French Syria and Lebanon. The Vichy government quickly named General Dentz High Commissioner of the Levant.

In June of 1941, General Dentz signed over Syria and Lebanon to the now occupying British military under his power as High Commissioner of the Levant.

At the conclusion of World War 2, General Dentz was deemed a traitor by the reestablished French government in Paris. He was sentenced to death for his crimes by the French government.

His sentence was reduced by now leader of the French government Charles de Gaulle, former leader of the Free French, to life in prison. General Dentz would die in French prison in 1945.

---

Helping General Dentz with managing the army of the Levant was French Lieutenant Joseph-Antoine-Sylvain-Raoul de Vedillac.

Lieutenant de Vedillac was General Dentz's second in command of the Army of the Levant. Lieutenant de Vedillac represented the Army of the Levant at the armistice talks with British and their allies.

---

It is unfortunate these last two gentlemen have very little information available to provide a better portrait of their participation in this battle.

However, I have a 'theory' of my own why this maybe. Conspiracy or not…you be the judge.

Over time, history has shown that to forget a person's existence one erases their names and any information about them. It has been known to be done in Egypt, Greece, Rome and countless other empires and governments.

This seems to be the case here as well. Determined to be traitors or war criminals at the conclusion of World War 2 many were left unmentioned and thusly forgotten about.

Surprising considering the leading nations in the surge of record keeping for near millennia were…we will just say in their regions.

# 3: THE WORLD IN 1941

The world by the middle of 1941 was succumbing to the reality that the war had spread to nearly every corner of the globe. A vast majority of the world's countries had either direct involvement in the war or indirect involvement in some capacity or another.

The countries that had direct involvement were troops on the ground, air, or sea for a defensive or offensive stance against their foreseen aggressors.

While the countries that had, indirect involvement was suppling war materials, food, or other aid to their allies. These countries had booming economies possibly a result of the aid they provided. Such as with later U.S. involvement.

In the Pacific, the Japanese military was heavily engaging the countries around them. The Japanese had become a formidable opponent.

The Japanese military was strategically overrunning countless island nations throughout the Pacific. Japan's forces were also engaged in land battles on the Korean peninsula and in eastern China.

The Japanese were quickly making their way around the Asian continent grabbing, land, resources and forced labor throughout. This massive threat had many nations in the region scrambling to deal with the Japanese military and their quick and silent expansion.

At the same time, things were not looking good for the

Russian government. Although not officially involved in the war they could recognize the warning sign, and it was not looking promising for the Russians.

The Russian government threatened by the Japanese fast expansion in the east and with the memory of the 1905 war still to recent to forget. The Russian government also felt the pinch from the west in the form of the German fast moving military.

Even with a non-aggression pact signed with Germany, the remembrance of World War 1. Russia knew it was going to be a matter of time before they became invested in the war.

Whether it was from the threat in the East or the one knocking on the door in the West. The answer for the Russians would come in June 1941 by way of the Nazi regime.

---

The United States were not directly involved in the war, but by the end of the year, were engaged in both the Pacific and European areas.

Prior to their direct involvement, the U.S. was the Allies' biggest supporter. The U.S. provided the British and her allies with not only war materials at a large rate, but other supplies as well.

Due to this demand by the Allies for American made supplies the economy was booming and became extremely profitable.

The U.S. was not only providing the British and its allies with the much-needed supplies but was also giving the British desperately needed intelligence and military information.

As Russia, the U.S. also had issues arising in the Pacific and their overseas territories that were closer to the threat of Japan.

The U.S. was attempting to make strides to strengthen the defenses of bases in the Pacific region against the inevitable attack posed by the Japanese military. Aligning with Allied forces gave them that tactical support.

---

In Europe, things were changing for all countries on the mainland. Italy under the guidance of Mussolini and his fascist government had become Germany's biggest ally and supporter.

Italy had an extensive military that was modernized and well equipped. It seemed as their military, large size, presented their enemies with an extraordinary task. However, it appears their bark was louder than their bite.

The tactics and training used by the Italian military was lacking but their sheer numbers made up some for this weakness. That said, the Italians led a large invading force in North Africa attempting to rout the British and the hold they had on the Suez Canal.

At the same time, the Italians did have territory beyond their borders. They controlled areas in the southern part of the European mainland and other interests they wished to maintain.

Germany, for all enemies, was the worst-case scenario. They had a huge, well-equipped, well-trained, and modernized military that utilized what was known as blitzkrieg war to quickly overrun and overwhelm their enemies.

By 1941, Germany had quickly and easily occupied

much of the European mainland including France in 1940, as previously mentioned and was setting up to expand even further.

By mid-year of 1941, Germany was planning a large invasion force along its eastern borders for an assault against Russia.

The Germans were battling the British anywhere they could including bringing the war to English soil with the German air force conducting bombing raids throughout southern and central England.

Germany had become the enemy no one wanted but everyone had to deal with in the western hemisphere.

France a long time bitter enemy of Germany had surrendered to the Nazi regime in 1940 and now fell under German control and occupation at a heavy cost to France.

During the occupation of France, Germany allowed the establishment of a government to keep French territories and the unoccupied zones functioning. The newly developed government became known as the Vichy French government.

The Vichy government was allowed to rule and make decisions for the unoccupied zones and territories as long as Germany agreed. This also previously mentioned…However, how would we get a better understanding of the two French governments.

The Vichy government in an effort to ease the cost of occupation and possibly to gain more freedoms from their German overseers began collaborating with Nazi Germany. Vichy government officials began promising military help and considerations of attacking Britain.

The collaborations between the Vichy government and the Germans included their use by the Germans and Italians of French held airbases and naval ports in French territories.

The French also allowed the Germans to use French factories to make military equipment for the Nazi German army as well as use of munitions already established not only in France but in their overseas territories as well.

Great Britain for their part found themselves almost alone in their attempt to rid Europe of the Nazi regime. The struggle for the British was becoming more difficult as time went on.

The Germans were doing air raids over southern and central England almost daily. The much-needed military supplies from the United States were becoming target points in the Atlantic by the German U-boat squadrons.

The supply chain was causing problems for Great Britain not only at home but also with its military stationed around the globe.

Britain was doing the best it could to relieve the threat of the air raids on English soil though not entirely successful.

The British military in North Africa was reeling with advancements made by Field Marshall Rommel. The British were throwing everything available to keep the Suez Canal from falling into German hands.

On the other side of the world, the British are finding themselves on the defensive against the fast moving hard pounding Japanese military of the Pacific.

The territories in the Pacific helped or protected by the

British were doing what they could to bolster up their defenses and halt the advancing Japanese military.

For the British and their vast empire are feeling the heat from powerful enemies around the world and seemingly doing it by themselves.

# 4 ISSUES

The British are facing insurmountable odds at every turn. They find themselves constantly surrounded by enemies everywhere around the globe.

This becomes a situation they must deal with sooner rather than later in the Middle East, not only in their own mandated territories but specifically in the Vichy French occupied territories of Syria and Lebanon.

The importance of the Middle East was not only for the oil reserves within the region, as some may believe. Communications, supplies, and the defense of the Suez Canal area become a priority for the British.

The Suez Canal area was vitally important to the British and Allies. The canal cut shipping between the Atlantic, Pacific, and Indian Oceans nearly in half. The Suez Canal allowed easy passage of shipping from the Atlantic through the Mediterranean Sea to the Red Sea into the Indian and Pacific Ocean. Eliminating the need to ship around the entire continent of Africa. This made shipping faster. Allowing the Allies to resupply and rearm their military around the globe at a fast rate.

British military intelligence and other agents become aware the German agents almost immediately flocked to the different French mandates to begin setting them up for German control and military uses. (13) Perceived as a threat British forces began to gather information to counter.

This knowledge and accusation by the British did hold some relevancy. There was a German document to the Embassy in Turkey that stated:

*"The French delegation informed the German Armistice*

*Commission that the French Government was yielding to our request for the granting of an entry permit for you in order to avoid giving the appearance of ill will, but that it maintained the standpoint that in view of the situation at the moment your coming was inopportune…"*
*"…The French Government requests that upon your arrival in Syria you contact High Commissioner General Dentz personally. The Foreign Minister requests that in carrying out your assignment you observe the following:*

1) *Your trip is purely of an informative nature. Its principle purpose is:*
   A) *To report on political and military situation in Syria, and as far as possible, the neighboring areas. Does England constitute a serious threat to Syria by way of Palestine? Are the resources of France adequate for defense? What progress is being made by the de Gaulle movement? What are the methods with which English propaganda is operating and what success does it have?*
   B) *To gather relevant data for our policy towards Arab states.*
   C) *To observe Germany's own interests of an economic and cultural nature and report on them.*

*You are requested to avoid, for your part, anything that might be construed as approval or support of tendencies directed at the French Government."* (14)

While the intelligence received by the British government was accurate in the sense of German agents in French territories. It was not however, as depicted by the British.

In all accounts, the German agents were not there for support or occupation but merely an information quest, at least that is the case to start out. It was later apparent the German agents in the area were attempting to spy on British territories and access any threats the British may pose to the area.

Unfortunately, for the British, German agents snooping around the French mandated territories was not their only concern.

After the conclusion of World War 1, the British government was given mandated territories in the Middle East by the League of Nations. The areas awarded to the British were Palestine, TransJordan, and Iraq.

Since becoming mandated territories of Britain, the people of these areas began revolting against the British. The British had promised them freedom and independence before the end of World War 1. Unfortunately, that is not exactly what they get.

With the British military and government, scrambling around their global empire the peoples of the British controlled territories in the Middle East used the distraction to fuel the anti-British animosity among the Arab citizens in the region.

In these Arab states, the leaders of the anti-British movements began reaching out to acquire help to rid themselves from under the heavy British thumb.

One telegram to the embassy in Italy states:

*The Iraq Minister of Justice, who is here again, presented via the Hungarian Minister, the urgent request that the Government of the Reich, too, associate itself in written form with the written declaration of the Italian Government regarding independence of the Arab states of Iraq, TransJordan, Palestine, and Syria. Only if there were a joint statement of the Axis Powers could the Iraq Government proceed to remove Foreign Minister Said and to foment immediately new disorders in Palestine..." "...The situation in Syria was very difficult because the English Consul was seeking to stir up French against the Petain Government and food supplies were extremely short."* (15)

The leaders of the Arab movement looking for independence anyway they could went with the age-old philosophy of "the enemy of my enemy is my friend".

This heightened threat within their own territories caused more stress on the British government and military of the region. It became another struggle that the British were faced with, by themselves.

For the leaders of the Arab movement their strategy of asking for Axis Power assistance will work for a short time. No consideration of consequence the Arab movement in the region does force the British to make tough decisions and act upon them. It was not only both mega-powers clashing for supremacy, but the people began to see the benefit to themselves with the evident opportunity to play both sides. That is apparent in many later discovered or released documents from rulers in these controlled areas.

The Grand Mufti, an Arab leader in the Middle East that had a very large following of people drafted a letter in January 1941 to Adolf Hitler; in the letter, he stated:

*"Excellency: England, that relentless and crafty enemy of the true liberty of people, had never tired of forging chains to enslave and subjugate the Arab people, sometimes in the name of a perfidious League of Nations and sometimes by flaunting false and hypocritical sentiments of humanity for the others, but always, in truth, for the most imperialistic designs camouflaged by the principles of democracy and of medacious internationalism…" "…the Arab people find themselves the center of the land and sea crossroads, which form, according to the English, the principle hub of "Imperial British Communications"…"…If the Arabs are aided in defeating Zionist aims, the Jews, and especially those of the United States, will be so demoralized at seeing the object of dream fade into nothingness that they will lose their enthusiasm for aiding Great Britain and will retreat before catastrophe…" "…the warmest sympathy of the Arab*

*peoples for Germany and the Axis is now henceforth an established fact…" "…the Arab peoples are everywhere and prepared to act, as is proper, against common enemy and to take their stand with enthusiasm on the side of the Axis to do their part in the well deserved defeat of the Anglo-Jewish Coalition."* (16)

The anti-British sentiment displayed and voiced by the leaders of the Arab movement like the Grand Mufti was believed to gain them assistance and aid from the Axis Powers in their goal to rid the Middle East of British Imperialism. The hope was to finally gain the freedom and autonomy promised yet never received.

A very passionate, emotion filled, and strategically worded call for help. I wonder if they speculated at all what the Axis Powers had in mind for those who needed a hand. Would they simply get an empty hand of promises or a bill…with a hefty price to pay?

It is one thing to live under the regime as they had waiting for promises to one-day be fulfilled. It is something entirely different to play both sides.

Sure this may have been considered best for the "short-term". On the other hand, one must question, what would come in the long-term? And…better for whom?

With growing resentment in the Middle East against the British, the collapse of the French government, and the establishment of the pro-Nazi Vichy government in France the enemies of the British were beginning to grow exponentially.

British officials in the Middle East were feeling like they were surrounded by a growing number of enemies. Sadly, for the British things were going to get 'worse before they would get better'.

Just eight days after the Grand Muftis letter to the Fuhrer, the Foreign Minister in Berlin received a telegram:

*"The Secretary General of the Grand Mufti will leave here day after tomorrow, first for Rome, since his visit there has been arranged by the Italian Minister at Baghdad. After a week stay he will go on to Berlin…" "…Nuri Said had resigned, with the cabinets approval. No announcement of this is to be made in order not to provoke the English unnecessarily. The Iraq government is now prepared to cooperate with us in everyway."* (17)

The realization that their pro-British government in Iraq was rapidly crumbling with the unexpected resignation of Nuri Said sent the British government reeling and scrambling for a viable solution.

The British were already spread incredibly thin not only in the region but also around the empire as a whole. They had no real resources to deal with this growing problem in Iraq.

For the next three months negotiations and diplomatic solutions were presented; all of them to no effective mutual results.

The Allies could not afford for the British to lose their footing in the Middle East. The British could definitely not lose their positions in the Middle East. The British mandated territories in the Middle East were vital to the British Empire.

Communications could flow easily from one end of their empire to the other, going through the Middle East. The Middle East gave the Allies control of the Suez Canal and it important shipping lanes. The British hold in the Middle East gave the Allies an oil reserve supply for their militaries.

Problems are going to keep compounding for the

British. The untimely resignation of Nuri Said and the political unrest with the British protectorate of Iraq along with the Grand Muftis communications and negotiations with Nazi Germany would not be the only concern for the British government.

To the shock of the British and their backers, in a short amount of time, the Vichy government had formed new governments in both Syria and Lebanon. This is thought to be done at the urging of Nazi Germany. (18)

This was an interesting turn of events considering recent communications between specific groups of people. It was also interesting in the speed in which the Vichy government reacted to the issue.

The Vichy overseers formed the new governments in Syria and Lebanon just in time. The majority leaders in both these countries were making plans to obtain independence from the noticeably weakened Vichy French government. The request for aid and hope for freedom instead led to an invasion of sorts…by a completely different 'enemy'.

Unlike the leaders of the anti-British movements in Iraq, the leaders and peoples of Syria and Lebanon did not relish in the idea that they could fall into the sphere of influence of Germany, Italy, or at the hands of the Vichy government.

The leaders and peoples of Syria and Lebanon, at the surrender of France to Germany and establishment of the Vichy French government, began plotting a way to avert German and Italian influence in the region. Unexpectedly, the Vichy government had acted faster than both the Syrian and Lebanese leaders had thought possible. (19)

For the British now there is the very real threat that

Axis Powers have a foothold in the Middle East and all its vital elements that are so important to hold the British Empire together and provide for its military.

# 5 BRITAINS VIEW

The British were not sure as what would happen after France had surrendered to the invading German military. The British position regarding issues with the Vichy French government and its mandated territories had been voiced and made public almost immediately after the surrender of France to Germany.

In July 1940, the British government issued a statement that they *"...could not allow Syria and Lebanon to be occupied by any other hostile or used as a base for attacks on countries in the Middle East."* (20)

According to Britain, her allies, the Arab leaders, Italy and of course Germany; Syria was the keystone to the Middle East. The British needed its presence in the Middle East especially during the war.

They relied on their presence in the region to quickly communicate across their vast empire. They were able to get supplies to their military personnel around the globe quickly by overland routes through the Middle East or in and out of the Suez Canal.

The British and their allies also used the area to get much needed supplies into Russia by way of Middle Eastern routes. The Allies desperately needed the oil fields in the region to keep the military machines moving fluidly against the Axis Powers.

The most important reason for the British to have a heavy presence in the region during the war was the much-needed Suez Canal that allowed easy transport of personnel, equipment, and supplies without having to go around the Horn of Africa.

The British knew that if the Germans became firmly

established within Syria they could accomplish three main objectives, all of them to great detriment to the Allied Powers war effort.

The first goal the Germans could accomplish could be a complete encirclement of Turkey.

Turkey had been attempting to remain a neutral party during the war. Prior to World War 2 breaking out on the European mainland Turkey had given the Allied Powers its backing, but that agreement had been given to France as part of the Alexandretta annexation and now France was under the helm of Nazi Germany.

This made the Allies wary as to which way the Turkey backing would fall. The British knew that if Germany was able to encircle Turkey it would give Axis Powers easy access to the Aegean Sea, the Balkans, Straights of Darnell, the Black Sea, and Southern Russia.

Having easy access to the areas would give the Germans and Axis Powers a complete circle around mainland Europe, by both land and sea. It would also give the Germans a larger front and more opportunity to invade Russia.

The second goal that the Germans could accomplish with a firm placement in Syria would be access to oil fields. From Syria, the Germans could march on the British mandated territory of Iraq and its heavy producing oil fields.

The Germans just like the British needed the oil for their heavily mechanized military. The British knew with the large anti-British movement in Iraq already established if the Nazi army decided to move into Iraq there would be a large local backing aiding the Germans in a route of the British from the area.

The empire that controlled the oil, controlled many things. This was important for many reasons, but mainly because this power equaled money.

The last goal, and the most feared by the British, if Germany gained strong presence in Syria would be a complete oust of British from the area all together. From Syria, the Germans could execute a grand slam on Palestine, TransJordan, and the much-desired Suez Canal.

This drive coupled with a strong push out of Libya would chase the British out of the Mediterranean Theatre of operations entirely. This would virtually cut the British Empire in half. (21)

The idea of a strong German presence in the Middle East was at the forefront of the British governments mind in 1941. Finally, towards the end of April 1941 the British Chiefs of Staff pointed out all the dangers that could exist by the Germans establishing a strong foothold inside Syria.

This idea and realization was something that General Archibald Wavell, British Commander in Chief of Middle East Forces, was keenly aware. It had been his reality longer than anyone else had.

The British Chiefs of Staff gave instructions to General Wavell to be prepared to send a force into Syria to aid any French resistance if the Germans tried to gain a strong hold in the region. (22)

The British government believed that they could stall, possibly forever, a Nazi movement into Syria if the British occupied the mandated territories of Syria and Lebanon by wrestling them from the Vichy government. (23) The British knew they could not take the Levant region from Germany but they could take it from the Vichy French and thwart any attempt by Germany or Axis Powers of invading the area.

The British were making plans and coming to terms with serious German threats to the Middle East by way of Syria. This idea had become engrained in the minds of the British government and British military in the Middle East.

However, for the British as they were planning to solve one problem, immediately another jumped into their laps. Their fears now realized.

The British government heads were sent spinning again on May 2, 1941 as the Iraqi revolt had begun. The Iraqi revolt was urged, funded, and supplied by Axis Powers by way of air bases in Syria.

A telegram to the German Foreign Minister states:

*"The Iraqi Minister read me a telegram from his government which just arrived. According to this, fighting began today between English and Iraq troops at the Habannyia airfield, and consequently war is in progress. Relations with England have been broken off..."*
*"...It also requests immediate military aid. In particular a considerable number of airplanes in order to prevent further English landings and to drive the English from the airfields. The English have a total of 8,500 troops on Iraq territory, including the recently landed forces, and the Iraqi have 50,000 men under arms. They want to raise another 50,000 and weapons for them are urgently needed..."* (24)

# 6 COLLABORATION

For the British it began to appear that they were being dealt harsh blows time after time. These hits to the British kept coming quicker and quicker with more impact each time.

It was feeling to the British that they were standing alone absorbing these hits. Whether the blows were coming by way of the Grand Mufti and his communication with Germany, the new Iraqi revolt, or the serious threat of German infiltration into Syria.

Not to mention the vast amount of problems plaguing the remainder of their empire. The British were constantly scrambling solving crisis after crisis.

Meanwhile, back in Syria, the Vichy government was adding fuel to the British fear of Vichy/German collaboration.

The British along with a few of their allies, including the United States, had believed the Vichy government was aiding the Germans more than other occupied countries. Now it was blatantly obvious to not only the British but also the rest of the world.

This kept the threat of a German presence in Syria very real for Britain and the Allies. In a memo from the German Director of the Political Department on May 9, 1941:

*"General Warlimont has been informed by the German Armistice Commission that according to a French report the Italian Government approached the French government for permission to use Syrian airfields for an Italian aircraft formation assignment for operationsl employment in Iraq..." "...It had been agreed with the French that the French government would not give a reply until the*

*German position has been stated…" "…it would seem to me that German operations by way of Syria would actually be endangered by simultaneous Italian action in that area."* (25)

The British were stunned at the blatant, documented cooperation by the French Vichy government to the Nazi German regime. For the British, they were not only contending with the Japanese expansionism throughout the Pacific region and now they had issues within their own territories too.

Boundaries thought to be etched in stone and long under their control with little difficulty. Now they were watching for enemies in all directions. Resources were becoming near scarce.

The Iraqi revolt was taking a lot of attention of the British military. On the European mainland and surrounding areas, including North Africa the British were dealing with the Axis Powers of Italy, Nazi Germany, and it appeared to the British to include now the Vichy French.

The idea of German/Franco collaboration became a real and viable threat for the British and was now on the forefront of all minds including the highest of officials.

In a recorded conversation between Adolf Hitler and Admiral Darlan of Vichy France, it was scribed that:

*"…Darlan welcomed this opportunity to stress once more the extent to which Marshall Petain and he himself were convinced of the need for the cooperation between France and Germany…" "…He pointed out since he joined the French government certain measures had been taken in agreement with Marshall Petain, especially in the economic field, which clearly supported the spirit of French collaboration with Germany. In this connection he referred to…" "…the airfields which were being made available in Syria…"*

The transcription of the recording further read:

*"The Fuhrer then also spoke about Iraq. Germany was about to oppose the English in Iraq. Germany was looking into the possibilities of doing this. He (the Fuhrer) would be interested in Darlan's opinion in the matter, especially with reference to the French forces stationed there. Darlan, who did appear well informed about the particulars, replied that there were approximately two divisions of French troops in Syria, but that they did not have any modern equipment. Furthermore numerous airfields were available..."*
*"...moreover, considerable stores of French aerial bombs were available. To be sure, France could not transfer any sizeable reinforcements to Syria, since the English from their bases at Cyprus would stop that transport..." "...Darlan repeated his offer to sell war materials to Iraq..." "...i.e. all rifles stocked up under Italian control as well as two thirds of all stores of arms and ammunition."*
(26)

Clearly obvious to myself, the British, that the Vichy government was beginning to take an active role in German domination, even in the Middle East.

With the Vichy government willing to sell arms and munitions to the rebels in Iraq. The opening up of airfields in Syria for Italian and German use.

The British, however, relations in the Middle East were going to continue to decline, and decline rather quickly.

A telegram from Paris to the German Foreign Minister, demonstrates the organization, planning, and preparation already in place. The telegram states:

*"In the negotiations regarding Syria/Iraq, the French government is prepared:*

1)  *To sell to Iraq up to three-fourths of all French war materials stored in Syria.*
2)  *To grant German and Italian aircraft the right to make immediate landings in Syria, to supply them within the*

35

*limits possible, and place at the disposal of the Luftwaffe and airfield north of Alep for its regular use.*

3) *To authorize the use of Syrian ports, highways, and railroads for shipments to Iraq and, in so far as practicable, provide protection by French vessels for German supply transports by sea from a point off Cyprus.*

4) *To train Iraq soldiers in Syrian territory in the use of the French weapons supplied.*

5) *To transmit to Germany reports received by the French High Command on English military forces and war measures in the Near East.*

6) *To comply with any other German demands for support of military operations in Iraq.*

*In consideration of these French contributions and with a view to strengthening Syria's defenses against England, which is also in Germany's interest, the High Command of the Wehrmacht is prepared, subject to the agreement of the Italian Armistice Commission, to authorize a number of measures for the military strengthening of Syria, which go beyond the terms of the Armistice Treaty."* (27)

Upon hearing of these agreements made by the Vichy government to that of Germany it appeared to the British that the Vichy French government had become a full fledge partner to Nazi Germany and shared their quests of domination at any cost.

# 7 VICHY PROMISES

The Middle East for the British had become a political hydra. They chop off one head, but two more grow in return. The British government was unable to contain one problem in the Middle East before another rose.

The world, especially Britain and her allies were left stunned and baffled. What was seemingly an easy transformation…the French government went from ally to enemy in less than one year.

The British were yet to receive another blow by the Franco/German collaboration efforts on the Middle East. In a signed document on May 27, 1941, the French and German governments agreed to not only the items declared in the May 24th document (previously mentioned) but the new agreement also declared that:

*"…2. In consideration of the situation in the Near East the High Command of the Wehrmacht agrees to the immediate execution of the following measures,…"*

A) *"Release of one-quarter of the total French war material stockpiled in Syria and the additional stocks to be left there according to a special agreement.*

B) *Transfer to Syria a heavy anti-aircraft battalion of 3 batteries with 5 issues of ammunition and 150 men from units released from metropolitan France. Replacement of these guns from supplies stored in metropolitan France.*

C) *Transfer to Syria of a light motorized anti-aircraft battalion with 150 men from units released in metropolitan France. Replacement of these guns from supplies stored in metropolitan France.*

D) *Transfer to Syria of twenty-four 25mm, anti-tank guns with 7,200 rounds of ammunition from supplies stored in metropolitan France.*

E) *Transfer to Syria twenty-four 75mm guns from supplies*

> *stored in metropolitan France. For the time being, these guns are to be stockpiled there again under Italian control. Release for combat is subject to the requirements of the situation.*
>
> F) *Transfer of 80 tons of materials (airplane parts).*
> G) *Transfer to Syria of 150 specialists from metropolitan France to reinforce the personnel of three fixed 75mm anti-aircraft batteries there.*
>
> *Regarding b to g: If, in exceptional cases, these or German supply transports to Syria go by sea, German forces will provide protection in the danger zone as far as the island of Kaseltorrizon, and by French from there to Syria. If the land route is used, the transports through German-controlled territory will be arranged by Germany.*
>
> H) *Transfer to Syria of a reinforced fighter group from North Africa, together with individual transport planes, with immediate landings at Brindisi, Athens, or Larissa, and Rhodes.*
> I) *Reinforcements of the air defenses of Syria by means of machine guns to be taken from the supplies released in accordance to point A.*
>
> *The High Command of the Wehrmacht is furthermore prepared in principle to supplement in so far as possible the supplies of gasoline and oil in Syria. If shipments are made by sea, the French transport ships in Greece and the escort units will be fueled in Greece, if necessary. For this purpose French tankers will be chartered to Germany in so far as possible."* (28)

To the eyes, minds, and hearts of the British government this agreement between the Germans and the Vichy French government, solidified Vichy France a willing combatant against Great Britain and her allies.

The British now see the mounting Franco/German collaboration details laid clearly. For the British it became vitally important that an effort needed to be made quickly in the Middle East or lose control.

The British knew they needed to act fast, or they would be squeezed out of the Eastern Mediterranean all together.

In Syria and Lebanon, the new established Vichy backed governments were under the direction and leadership of General Dentz. The same man that surrendered Paris to the invading Nazi German forces in June of 1940.

General Dentz's and the whole of the Vichy government's failure to resist German demands coupled with the agreements and protocols signed by both German and Vichy French governments kept piling up for the British. Ultimately giving the British government and military the opportunity to claim that the German government and military was preparing to install themselves in the French mandated territory of Syria. (29)

To the British, the Allies and the world by all accounts and observations that is what appeared to be taking place.

The Vichy government and General Dentz had a well-known reputation for promising the Allies that they were a separate independent country with the ability to make their own decisions, and can resist German demands.

However, to the Allies, especially the British, the Vichy government were obviously feeble and willing to appease the German government at every demand.

To the British and the Allies the promises and words spoken by the Vichy government could not be trusted as their actions showed different then the words spoken.

# 8 BRITAIN'S MOVE

Syria was now in the spotlight, not just for the British and their allies, but also for the Vichy government and the Axis Powers.

The Allies knew that Syria and Lebanon was going to be a test case for the Vichy government's collaboration policy with the German High Command.

This was also going to be a test for the British. To see if they had the ability to prevent a complete German domination of the Eastern Mediterranean. (30)

They are only aware of the most obvious threats. Will halting one stop all threats or are more waiting behind the scenes?

General Wavell (British High Commander of all Middle Eastern Forces) knew that the Vichy French forces in Syria were in the process of becoming resupplied. He was aware of this monitoring recent activity in the Syrian ports and air bases. Witnessed by British military personnel that reported in.

The British government made General Wavell aware of the agreements and protocols intercepted between the Vichy government and the German High Command. Making the threat from Syria for General Wavell and his command immediate and dangerous.

With that intercepted documentation, General Wavell knew that the Vichy forces were now going to be well armed and equipped, backed by over 90 tanks with artillery. (31)

The beginning of May 1941 the British decided it was time to make the first move towards Syria and the Vichy government in control.

The British knew the ease of which the Vichy forces in Syria could be reinforced and resupplied by the vast amounts of shipping ports in the area. The British had seen a continuous increase in activity in the Syrian ports.

It was just a matter of time before they put their plan into play. In an effort to slow the shipments into Syria, slowing resupply and reinforcement lines, the British navy declared a mine zone blockading the Syrian ports. This move by the British made access to Syria by sea virtually impossible. (32)

Not long after the British blockade, sounding doubtful of efforts, and seeming to challenge or possibly support the attack of French government on the other, Prime Minister Winston Churchill wrote to General Auchinleck (a British Commander in the Middle East) on May 14, 1941.

*"...Even less can we attempt to dominate Syria at the present time, though the Free French may be allowed to do their best there."* (33)

Churchill was referring to the Free French forces that were in the Middle East aiding the British against the Axis Powers.

The Free French forces did not recognize or support the Vichy government in France at all. Instead existing under the leadership of General Charles de Gaulle and his exiled French government housed, supported, and officially recognized by the British government.

General de Gaulle and his Free French government held to the same ideas and principles of the original French government before the surrender to Germany. Principles possibly responsible for their ability to reorganize anywhere at any time.

The Free French refused to recognize the armistice signed between France and Germany in 1940. Still bringing the fight to the Axis Powers the best they could. They were loyal and a true ally to the British, aiding them throughout the war in Europe.

Prime Minister Churchill knew the taking of Syria from the hands of the Vichy government was vitally important to the safety of the region. He was also keenly aware that his forces in the Middle East were spread extremely thin.

The British forces in the Middle East were already struggling to fight down the large revolt in their own territory of Iraq. Probably his reason for mentioning the Free French specifically in his letter to General Auchinleck.

The forces in the region were fighting two separate brutal campaigns in North Africa protecting the control of the Suez Canal, and fighting a campaign occupying the island of Cyprus. Cyprus was also vital for shipping and the air forces of the region.

The vast amount of campaigns and the large-scale revolt in Iraq was taking their toll on the Allied forces in the Mediterranean Theatre. The British were being spread thin around the world facing numerous enemies.

The lifeline of resupply ships coming from the United States under constant threat from German U-boats in the open seas put much strain on the British. They were running low on reinforcements and supplying all their forces was becoming an unsurmountable task.

Prime Minister Churchill knew there was no reasonable way the British could muster an army force large enough to take over and occupy Syria at the moment. Aware that action was needed in Syria but at a loss as how to proceed with the next course of action.

However, things for the British in the region were quickly going to change.

On the evening of May 18, 1941 General Catroux (Free French Commissioner in the Middle East) informed General Wavell that he had gained intelligence on movement inside Syria.

According the information intercepted by General Catroux, the Vichy French government in Syria was withdrawing all their troops into Lebanon, and were handing the whole of Syria over to Germany for their own occupation.

The intelligence gathered by Catroux stated that the road to Damascus was open and undefended. General Catroux told General Wavell that it was urgent to take advantage of the opportunity and send a force into Syria immediately before the German troops arrived. (34)

Previous experience with Free French intelligence and the British command had taught General Wavell to take any information provided by the Free French with caution. The Free French had already proven to be a good strong ally for the British but they were known to be reckless in their decisions.

They would not spend time enough verifying and gathering more data before making rash decisions. The Free French forces and some British had found themselves in a few precarious positions before based on the information gathered, analyzed, and attacked with the patience of research and perfect planning by the Free French.

General Wavell with his cautious mindset regarding the intelligence he was provided by General Catroux attempted to verify and confirm the information. Wavell used other intelligence sources in the area but was unable to prove or disprove the information provided to him by General Catroux. (35)

Adequately General Wavell not being able to confirm the information provided by the Free French, refused to act based solely on General Catroux intelligence report.

Instead of acting on the information provided by the Free French, General Wavell decided to call a meeting for the next day May 19, 1941. To discuss the intelligence given to him by General Catroux with his command force.

General Wavell also wanted to address the growing problems and concerns associated with Syria, the Vichy government and its collaboration with Germany.

General Wavell discovered during the course of this meeting that his command had an overwhelming consensus to the necessity of stalling the Germans before they could fully occupy the Vichy French mandated territory. (36) But for General Wavell and the Allies was this the best or only answer for now?

During the meeting with the Allied Middle Eastern Commanders, General Wavell reported General Catroux's information to the British Chiefs of Staff back in England. He wanted the British High Command to have the most recent information possible on the Vichy French situation in the Middle East.

After General Wavell informed the British Chiefs of

Staff of the latest developments in the area they reiterated the point that some type of immediate action needed to take place in Syria. (37)

General Wavell knew something had to happen. However, he had two big problems. The 'when' and 'where' to take action, and 'how' with such depleted resources?

Two days after General Wavell's meeting with the Allied Middle Eastern Commanders and the reiteration by the British Chiefs of Staff, General Catroux traveled to Palestine on May 21, 1941.

Catroux was scheduled for a meeting with a French officer from Syria. The information provided to General Catroux during the course of this meeting gave him revelations and sent his mind racing with panic.

At the closure of his meeting General Catroux sent an urgent message to General Wavell, admitting to him that the information he provided on May 18th was completely incorrect.

General Catroux warned Wavell the exact opposite of, his earlier information was the real plan.

Catroux learned that rather than the Vichy French forces withdrawing into Lebanon, the Vichy were in fact moving troops south into Damascus. These troop movements south towards Damascus provides a defensive position in and around the various routes leading into the city.

Based on his newly acquired information General Catroux told General Wavell that nothing short of a large invasion force could attempt to occupy Syria. (38) But, was that something they could accomplish at this time?

The idea of a large invasion force was General Wavell and the Allied Commanders of the Middle East's most important challenge. Time was brief, resources were in short supply, and much was at risk anyway you looked at the possible outcomes.

# 9 ORGANIZING

Armed with this new more accurate information provided by General Catroux, General Wavell and the Allied Command of the Middle East backup a few steps.

For Wavell this step back is not going to last. He is being constantly urged by the British Chiefs of Staff back in England to organize something to address the concern in Syria.

Well apprised of the need to contain the situation inside Syria, General Wavell and his command faced two great difficulties in forming an invasion force to occupy Syria.

The first of the difficulties, the easier of the two, were gathering enough transport and signals for the invading force.

General Wavell knew as most military commanders do, that a great invasion force would be almost inept if they could not be moved efficiently or if communication was nearly non-existent.

The second difficulty General Wavell faced, and the most serious, was being able to scrape together enough soldiers to produce an invasion force of any magnitude. (39)

General Wavell and the British Middle East forces were already knowingly short on manpower and equipment with the several ongoing campaigns and revolts taking place in multiple locations.

The idea and task of putting another force together for yet another campaign seemed like an almost impossibility.

Despite the difficulties and setbacks General Wavell began, the tremendous task of organizing his forces for an invasion into Vichy French held Syria. He immediately located, armed, and began issuing orders to the forces he had available.

---

The 7th Australian Division had been moved, General Wavell sent orders to them to move into Northern Palestine and wait to be rearmed and resupplied there.

During the same time, Wavell sent orders to the 5th Indian Infantry Brigade to move to the northern frontier territory of TransJordan.

After he got the 7th Australian Division and the 5th Indian Infantry Brigade, moving to the north General Wavell then issued orders to General Wilson (British Commander of Palestine) to begin making preparations for an advance into Syria. (40)

Needing all the help and troops he could get his hands on General Wavell sent a message to General Catroux, and the Free French forces stationed in Egypt asking them to move to Palestine to aid in the invasion of Syria.

The Free French forces had been in Egypt aiding the British in the defense of the area and the Suez Canal against the relentless German army.

General Catroux, already having been stationed and lived in Syria prior to World War 2, and his Free French forces hurriedly made their way into Palestine to aid in the invasion of Vichy held Syria.

---

On May 25, 1941, General Wavell reported to the

British War Office that he and his staff were making preparations for a planned advance into Syria. Informing the British Chiefs of Staff that the advance included Free French forces.

The remnants of the decimated 4th Calvary Division, plus other various mixed Divisions and groups at his immediate disposal.

General Wavell also informed the War Office that he had great concern and reservations about using Free French forces in the initial invasion of Syria.

He believed that the presence of the Free French on Syrian soil would stiffen the resistance of the established Vichy French forces in Syria. He knew that the Free French were seen as traitors in the eyes of the Vichy French government and military. (41)

Although concerned, he was ready to fight with those available. His greatest concern was the potential and loss they faced bringing the Free French into this fight. What would their enemies do to those they saw as 'traitors' to their own people?

# 10 THE PLAN

General Wavell and the Allied Commanders of the Middle East had a well-thought and very detailed plan for the invasion of Syria.

The plan was to invade and attack the Vichy French forces fast on multiple fronts before they could be resupplied reinforced or mounts any measureable counter attacks.

General Wavell and his commanders wanted to make the Syrian invasion, as quick as possible. They knew that a prolonged engagement would cost the Allied Middle Eastern forces more than they could afford to give.

The first prong of the invasion force was to come on the right flank by the 5th Indian Brigade. Their objective was to advance and occupy Deraa and the rail line of the Yarmuk Railway.

The control of the railway stopped the Vichy French forces from being able to use it to move troops and supplies through the country in bulk.

It also gave the British the opportunity to utilize the rail lines for their own purposes and objectives.

The second prong of the attack was going to come at the hands of the Free French. At the same time the 5th Indian Brigade was moving on Deraa and the rail ways the Free French had the objective of going straight through to Damascus.

The Free French were to engage and occupy the city. First though they had to wrestle it from the hands of the Vichy forces there.

The last report received by General Wavell was from the Free French General Catroux that stated the Vichy forces were making an effort to strengthen the defenses in and around the city of Damascus. Which would impeded the 5th Indian Brigade.

The third prong of the invasion was to come from the 7th Australian Division. From their posts in Northern Palestine, the 7th Australian Division was to advance into Syria in two columns. The first column was to occupy the area in and around Marjayun, while the second column advanced up the coast towards Beirut.

Advances by the 7th Australian Division up the coast were made to cut off the coastal ports to the interior of the country. Rendering any troops or armament caches stocked up in the ports useless to the Vichy French forces on the ground. (42)

General Wavell and his command also put together implementations to use the British Royal Navy in the invasion of Syria. It was decided that as the British led invasion force advanced deep into the heart of Syria the British Royal Navy was to support the advance from off the coast.

The Royal Navy was to dispatch a squadron off the coast that was to parallel the ground troops moving north into the country offering the ground troops support and cover for their advancements.

Knowing there are limits of available fighter planes, General Wavell and his commanders decided it best to use the few airplanes they had available, to provide air support for the Royal Navy in case of any enemy air attacks. (43)

Knowing the difficulties faced by General Wavell and the Allied Middle East Command, Prime Minister Winston

Churchill talked before the British Parliament in May 1941 and was quoted:

*"In Syria resources are equally strained. The Commanders-in-Chief of the Middle East had said that the maximum force that could be spared for Syria until the Australians were re-equipped was one mechanized cavalry brigade, one regiment of artillery, and one infantry battalion, subject that they were not needed for a commitment in Iraq. This force could not be expected to deal with the number of troops which the Germans would be able to dispatch to Syria, and should not be sent unless the Vichy French were actively resisting. If it was decided to advance into Syria it would certainly be better that the troops be British in first instance and not Free French, whose intervention would be bitterly resented."* (44)

This is about the only time in which Prime Minister Churchill agrees with General Wavell on a subject.

Both agreeing that the Middle East Command is lacking personnel, and supplies for an invasion and occupation of Vichy Syria.

Churchill also in agreement the idea of using Free French soldiers in the initial invasion would not be a good idea and would make the Vichy French in Syria resentful and resist that much more desperately.

Their strained political and military relationship apparent overtime between the two gentlemen. However, in this instance, truly what may have been best was considered before greedy agendas for power.

# 11 AMERICA'S VOICE

The United States for their part was not officially involved in the war. They had no real military commitment to anyone or anywhere at this time. Until the strike at our soul, December 7, 1941, the bombing of Pearl Harbor.

However, the United States had a very heavy hand already in the war, especially in Europe. They were consistently feeding the British with as much intelligence reports as they could.

In addition to that, the United States was supporting the British with armaments, supplies, and munitions to fight the war. So technically,we were the peacekeepers...the defenders.

United States General Dwight D. Eisenhower stated that:

*"The Middle East, with its vast oil resources, was still another region whose safety was important to America. It provides one of the avenues by which supplies might be sent to Russia..."* (45)

Backing up for a moment...this statement is important for the U.S. to add their two cents. The U.S. 'protecting' this avenue, aligned with other events in the world concurrent with the situation developing in Syria.

The U.S. was suppling Russia, by ways of the Middle East routes, with armaments and munitions. Russia was attempting to build up its military presence along its borders with Nazi controlled Europe. The German military had been amassing a large army in the area.

Russia had a large military force, but their factories could not produce enough supplies fast enough for them. The U.S. supplies were vital for Russia and its defense, which would come quickly.

In June 1941, Hitler and the German war machine from their amassed troops against the Russian borders launched a full on invasion into the heartland of Russia. The invasion, known as Operation Barbarossa, led to the death of nearly 20 million Russian soldiers and citizens.

The U.S. supplies into southern Russia became a lifeline for the Russian military to mount any resistance to the fast moving German military.

For the United States, to announce to the world the importance of keeping the supply lines to Russia open through the Middle East helped solidify Russia as an ally against a common enemy.

Watching the events unfold in Europe and the Middle East. Knowing the extent of the Vichy French collaboration with Germany. The United States was being mindful of its words and actions in the wake of the recent events.

The United States Secretary of State Cordell Hull indicated his fear of the seemingly extensive Vichy French concessions to Germany. Hull declared that any move of this sort:

*"…would at once place France in subservience, and would also make her part, the instruments of aggression against other peoples and nations…"*

The statement made by Secretary Hull, was quickly answered, and rebuked by the Vichy French government.

In Le Tempe (a French newspaper), the Vichy government made strong assurances that under no circumstances or conditions would France join Germany on aggressions made towards other countries. (46)

An even more interesting document. Nothing as any other information and completely not matching their actions.

A rebuttal was offered by the Vichy French government and taken lightly since they had had already shown the Allied Powers differently.

If any doubt lingered about the Vichy French policy of collaborating with the Reich, that vanished on June 10, 1941.

That day Darlan (Vice Premier of Vichy France) broadcast a speech throughout France, speaking for Petain (Premier of Vichy France), speaking to the French people. Darlan argued for the necessity of collaborating with Germany as the only alternative to national suicide. (47)

This open broadcast speech by Darlan showed the United States and especially the British to what extent the Vichy French government admittedly was willing to go to appease the German government. To appear righteous to their people.

In response to Darlan, Secretary of State Hull again stepped forward to voice United States opinion of the situation. This time with a strongly worded statement.

Hull points to the German use of Syrian airbases as evidence of the lengthy union (the bases used during the Iraqi revolt and the bombing of Cyprus):

*"...that the German military effort is making use of France and that the German initiative in Syria is resulting in conflict, not only France against Britain but Frenchmen against Frenchmen..."*

That later part of the statement, most hard hitting. A country divided and so many displaced, or gone from this earth. Yet, there is little documentation about these specific efforts though the impact was huge. Why?

As far as Darlan's appeal to the French people, Secretary Hull insisted that it was preposterous for him to expect Hitler to grant more favorable terms, just because they bend to his will.

*"...should the conquered peoples prostrate themselves and bestow upon him unrestrained license to deal as he may see fit with their lives, their liberties, and their entire welfare..."* (48)

This sudden openness by the Vichy French government about involvement. It was clear, to the world that there was a very real threat by way of Syria. This was no longer theory or guessing. This was real and the time for patient planning or over analyzing is long over.

For the British and their allies in had become no longer an 'if' to advance into Syria but a 'when' to advance into Syria.

However, two problems plagued and stalled the British about Syria. Would they be able to assemble enough troops as these governments scraped for each man they sent?

Question two, should the Allies use Free French troops in the initial invasion? This was the 'gentlemen's war'. It was never about brute force or weaponry used. (At least by the Allies standards) It was political power, savvy, and strength backing numbers.

It was about intimidation and the respect or fear drawn by using a single but powerful name.

# 12 THE NEXT MOVE

Wrestling Syria away from the Vichy French was now beyond any doubt a necessity for the Allies. The problem that had been known for some time was assembling a force large enough to do so.

Given the known issues, General Wavell did what he could to gather his invading forces and planned all resources the best he could.

General Wavell's and the Allied forces spread thin throughout various campaigns and revolts had been taking place in and around the Middle East for quite some time. They were the only troops deployed in this region. These were the conditions nearly worldwide.

Despite the personnel shortage General Wavell faced he managed to gather a Syrian invading force faster than originally hoped.

Joined by British Major General John Bagot Glubb with his TransJordan Arab Army, General Wavell also assembled British and Scottish regulars from various units around the Middle East.

Along with these soldiers, the resourceful Wavell pulled together Anzacs, Canadians, Indians (mostly Sikhs and Gurkhas), and Free French, Australians, New Zealanders, and Free Czechoslovakian soldiers. (49)

Almost miraculous as all seemed to fall into place just as it needed to.

On the other side of the border in Vichy Syria, the Vichy military was faring slightly better organizing their forces. The Vichy forces in Syria were backed by Senegalese, Annamites, Algerians, Moroccans, Lebanese, and Vichy loyal French regular soldiers. (50)

All keeping this a numbers game and a potentially still difficult battle ahead. Unity and skill will matter.

The colorful cast of characters that General Wavell and his command had assembled was truly something to behold. The force for the Syrian invasion was literally a hodgepodge of soldiers, units, and countries from around the globe.

Just a few days before the invasion began an Australian Brigadier General told a United States war correspondent *"This is going to be a mixed show."* (51)

He was apparently referring to the mixed military force that General Wavell and the Middle East Command had assembled.

Now, these men are to charge into battle...this battle...a unit with one shared goal. Their goal clear and consistent. Their enemy's motive even clearer with time.

In Beirut, at this time a Vichy French captain told United States War Correspondent Peters *"We are fighting for the King of Prussia."* (52)

The Vichy captains comment as reported by Peters was just another example of the flaunting, arrogant mentality of the Vichy forces. It also clarified that the Vichy government was giving backing to the Nazi regime.

This statement showed the world that not only was the Vichy government but its military as well, backed the Axis Powers. This Vichy captain as reported by Peter's referred to Adolf Hitler as the 'King of Prussia', showing him respected and honored among the Vichy soldiers.

This gave more credence to the British and Allies

position about doing something regarding the rising situation in Syria.

Regardless of the decisions and plans set. British, problems were rapidly escalating with no forces moving, yet.

However, the British decide to make another move towards the invasion of Syria.

On June 4, 1941, the British Royal Air Force bombarded oil tank reserves and the water front defenses in and around Beirut. This done at the thought of the British to slow the flow of oil for Vichy forces and the Axis Powers but to also begin to soften up defenses ahead of the ground forces invasion into the territory.

The bombardment by the Royal Air Force did slow the moving of oil from the reserves to the Axis and Vichy forces. The damage was quickly repaired and oil again moving to its desired locations.

In response to the British bombardment in the Beirut the Vichy French the next day, June 5, 1941, conducted an air raid on Amman the capital of the British mandated territory of TransJordan. (53)

Besides being the capital Amman held no military significance for the British, there was no large number of troops stationed in the city and no munitions supply to speak of.

This attack was just a retaliatory venture perpetrated by the Vichy French. Their air force in the area was lacking armaments and any real goal in mind. It was done out of spite and retaliation.

On June 8, 1941, British led ground forces and Free French forces crossed the border into Syria. (54)

The United States again weighed in on the issue, Secretary of State Hull made a statement on June 13, 1941:

*"From the standpoint of the French people and others who have a love for freedom and have freedom the attitude of the present Government of Vichy is a matter of the deepest disappointment."* (55)

Hull in his statement was ridiculing the Vichy government's decisions to collaborate with the Axis Powers. He was also appalled at the flaggurent disregard the Vichy government was with the rights and liberties of their own citizens.

# 13 UNITED STATEMENTS

In the early morning hours of June 8, 1941, the British led "rag tag" force crossed the borders into Syria. The ground forces were advancing on the already planned out four prong assault through Syria.

The 5th Indian Infantry advancing out of TransJordan on their way to Deraa and to occupy the Yarmuk railways.

The British has the 7th Australian Division split in two prongs one to engage at Marjayun and the other marching up the coast to Beirut.

The Allies also had the Free French forces coming out of Palestine to engage the heavily defended area of Damascus.

The original plan had changed very little except for the use of the Royal Air Force to start the invasion.

The Royal Air Force would take a hard punch at the air bases in both Syria and Lebanon with the few planes at their disposal. The effort was to limit the use of the airfields and Vichy Air Force against the four prongs of the ground invasion forces. The only other defense at this time.

When the ground forces crossed the borders into Syria early that morning the British Royal Navy dispatched a squadron along the coast routes of Syria and Lebanon. This squadron began heavily bombarding coastal defense positions throughout both Syria and Lebanon, especially around the city of Beirut. (56)

Sir Henry Wilson (British General) headed north out of Palestine towards Beirut with the two prongs of 7th Australian Division. The two columns joined up around the city of Tyre and battled back and forth with Vichy forces that put up stiff resistance for three days at Sidon. (57)

On June 10 1941, Prime Minister Churchill in a statement in the House of Commons:

*"...Now I come to the Syrian operation. Let me repeat that we have no territorial designs in Syria or anywhere else in French territory. We seek no colonies or advantage of any kind for ourselves in this war. Let none of our French friends be deceived by the blatant German and Vichy propaganda. On the contrary, we shall do all in our power for the freedom, independence and right of France. I have, in a letter which I wrote to General de Gaulle, said "the rights and greatness of France"; we shall do all in our power to restore her freedom and her rights, but it will be for the French to aid us in restoring her greatness. There can be no doubt that General de Gaulle is a more zealous defender of France's interests than are the men of Vichy, whose policy is that of utter subservience to the German enemy.*

*"It did not take much intelligence to see that the infiltration into Syria by the Germans and their intrigue in Iraq constituted very great dangers to the whole Eastern flank of defense in the Nile Valley and the Suez Canal. The only choice before us in that theater for some time had whether, at heavy risk in delay, to prepare a considerable force, as we have done. It was also necessary to restore the position in Iraq before any serious advance in Syria could be made. Our relations with Vichy and the possibilities of an open breach with the Vichy Government evidently raised the military and strategic significance of these movements to the very highest point."* (58)

Prime Minister Churchill in his address to the House of Commons he wanted the people of Britain to understand and know why the invasion of Syria became a focal point. He also wanted the people of France to know that neither Britain nor the Allies wanted anything from France other than to help get them restored to the prestigious place they were before the war began.

For their part, the United States issued another statement regarding the situation in Syria, Secretary of State Cordell Hull stated:

*"When Germany recently desired to make use of Syria to attack British forces in Iraq no objection much less resistance, to this action was made by France, although the terms of the armistice between France and Germany did not require that France permit territory under French control outside occupied France to be used as a base for German military operations, and Marshall Petain declared as recently as a few weeks ago that he would not permit such use. The use of Syria is vitally important part of the general plan of Hitler to invade Iraq, Egypt and the Canal area, and Africa. When the Vichy authorities in Syria, acting under the Vichy government, made no effort to prevent German use of Syria as a military base, and when they permitted even the shipment from Syria of military supplies of French manufacture to be used by the Germans against France's former ally, they permitted Germany to extend the theater of war not French mandated territory. To resist this further expansion of German aggression the British forces in the Near East entered Syria to prevent German actions there which the French, under direction of the Vichy government, were permitting if not abetting. Yet the French authorities in Syria have considered it necessary to contest bitterly this British effort to prevent Syria from being used as a German base. These facts unmistakably demonstrate that the German initiative in Syria is resulting in conflict, not only France against Britain but Frenchmen against Frenchmen. Germany seems to have prevailed on the Vichy government to do Germany's fighting in the Syria area of the general German advance."* (59)

In his statement, Secretary Hull wanted to assure the British and Allies that the United States was backing and supporting the cause to invade Syria. He was also publicly criticizing the Vichy French government on a world stage.

The Secretary, as Churchill in his statement, wanted the

Vichy government to know that to the world they are seen as co-conspirators with the Nazi regime and how appalling it is for the world to know that the Vichy French are actually putting up fierce resistance to the occupying forces led by the British into Syria.

Although Churchill's statement was more passionate towards the French. Encouraging those to fight for a better government. Restore the country to what it was before. However, both were very clear on intent, or so it seemed.

# 14 INVASION BEGINS

It was the initial hopes of the British and Allies that making a move into Syria would be met with little to no resistance by the hands of the Vichy French in the territory. The British had told a United States War Correspondent they hoped that the objectives in Syria would be taken *"...with a view to obviating needless strife and bloodshed."* (60)

That hope quickly diminished as the British led invasion made their way into the Vichy French held territories. A wonderful plea to end the savage fighting. When it was known numbers would be dwindling.

General Wavell and the Middle East Command had decided to place British General Sir Henry Maitland Wilson in charge of the infiltration of Syria and Lebanon. (61) That decision was a strong one as General Wilson had spent most of his already long military career in various countries and territories.

An experienced leader, seemingly more understanding and sympathetic to the native cultures and people of foreign countries. General Wilson not known to be a warmonger jumping into fierce battles blindly.

He made calculated decisions to minimize casualties amongst his men, citizens, and even enemies.

With what had been assembled for this surge, great care needed to be shown. The region they were betting to control needed protection as well as the people in the fight. The Allies knew that any campaign into Syria needed handled very tenderly for two very specific reasons.

The first reason was due to the Arab population not only in Syria but also throughout the Middle East. There was already resentment of foreign occupation in the region among many native peoples and the revolt in Iraq still raging on. Any further prodding against the Arab peoples could be devastating to the British tasks at hand.

To the Arab population and other cultures the city of Damascus in Syria was considered to be the "Pearl of the East" and taking of the city needed to be handled gingerly to not anger an already volatile local Arab population.

The second reason the Allies needed to handle this invasion tenderly, (specifically for the British) was the French Navy in ports around the Mediterranean area.

The British knew that if French public opinion were sufficiently roused by the Syrian invasion, the Vichy French government could be encouraged to use its remaining naval fleet, in particular, their submarines against the British Royal Navy. (62)

The use by the Vichy French of their navy was a true concern for the British. With resources limited to only ground troops and few planes, the activation of their navy could have proven costly to the British.

The British had already attacked the French Navy in their homeports. In June of 1940, around Morocco the British attacked and sunk French naval vessels and damaged several more while killing nearly 1,300 French sailors.

The French navy was a viable threat the British were concerned and could have wiped them out quickly. This battle would end in the favor of the Axis Powers and the British could maintain no hold.

The Allied campaign into Syria had been divided into four different assaults and objectives to best utilized troops and mitigate their damage.

Heading up from the south out of Palestine, British led troops would split into two columns. One striking a route up the coast heading for Beirut. The second column would take a more inland approach to take the city and area around Marjayun, and then continue on to Beirut.

Also leaving Palestine, the Free French forces would march towards Damascus and occupy the city and area around.

From the east out of TransJordan, the British led troops headed for Deraa and the vital Yarmuk rail line at the same time these forces would go for Palmyra.

Once these objectives had been successfully accomplished, the forces would then head to the areas of Aleppo and Latakia. (63)

---

The initial wave of the British invasion moved quickly and they made good headway proving their plan had hopes of success. The four-prong attack against the Vichy French forces left them scrambling for defensive positions and standings. The Allies plan strong and apparently unexpected.

Three days after the start of the invasion on June 11, 1941 members of the Vichy French government met with members of the German Embassy to discuss the situation in Syria. The invasion proving so successful it was now the time to regroup or change plans. The Vichy French forces were losing traction rapidly.

The French representatives had informed the German Embassy members:

*"...it [Syrian Army] is ready to sacrifice itself in a struggle against English attacks, hopeless though it may be,..."*

*"…The native Arabs are basically anti-foreign; however, as a result of the favoring of the Jews by the English and because English action in Iraq, their dislike of England may be counted on to outweigh their dislike of France."*

*"…the French Government very urgently request military relief for Syria through German air attacks on Haifa and a bombing of the very numerous units of the British fleet cruising off the Syrian coast or heading for Syria…"*

*"…the French Government is willing to resort to reprisals against English bases like Gibraltar, Freetown, and Bathurst on account of the English attack on Syria…"* (64)

The Vichy French government seemed to be aware that their efforts to keep the English out of Syria would be a futile attempt. Nonetheless, they still kept a positive attitude and gave reassurances to the German government while asking for military assistance. Their plea was the best option to stomp the Allied threat fast.

For this military assistance, the Vichy French offered new concessions to the Nazi regime by way of attacking other British held points. All aid offered only with a price to pay even with the Vichy French sworn allegiance.

The perspective of the Vichy French, this was offered not only as a thank you to the German government. However, the Vichy French were looking to gain some retribution for what it saw as an unwarranted invasion into their mandated lands.

The German perspective, they expend no unnecessary resources without some reward.

The Syrian invasion by the Allies brought the Franco/German collaboration closer. In doing so, the Vichy French all but pledged their loyalty to the German quest for domination in the region. Their pleas heard and meeting fruitful.

The closer collaboration between the Vichy French government and the German government proved what Britain knew all along, and the Vichy deceived about its 'need' for relations with Germany. It became evident not only in previous actions the Vichy relied on their collaboration. Although, sow on the battle field the Vichy government relied heavily of the Reich for all matters whether political, militaristic, or internal.

Their pledge of allegiance now coming at a great cost. The bindings to the Reich tightening with each plea and promise.

---

Regardless of the situation of the Vichy government or their policies and agreements with Germany, the British led forces in Syria pressed on.

At the city of Sidon, the Australian army wrestled it from the Vichy defenders. The victory short lived, for they quickly lost the city again to a ferocious counter attack led by General Dentz himself (the man who surrendered Paris a year earlier).

As a result of this huge counter attack by General Dentz and his Vichy forces the Allied British Royal Navy headed in and pounded Sidon and Vichy defenses around the city with their large weapons.

The Royal Navy continued this heavy bombardment while being heavily attacked by Axis bombers from the area. The Australian ground forces while waiting for the navy onslaught to soften the defenses around the city shot down three German fighter planes that had Italian markings. (65)

This showed British command in the area that not only was Germany aiding the Vichy French government...but also all Axis powers were ready to offer aid and involvement.

The British Royal Navy had dramatically softened the defensive positions in and around Sidon, and the Australian ground forces moved in, easily seizing and securing the city from the Vichy French troops.

After ensuring the city of Sidon was secure, the Australians continued heading north up the coast to the outskirts of Beirut as planned.

The British Navy kept up a non-stop heavy bombardment of the city of Beirut, and all its defensive positions. Clearing the path for continued Allied advancement. This continued for the better part of week before the Australian Divisions arrived on the outskirts. (66)

The ground attack plan for the British and their allies had changed little since its inception. The Australian division coming out of Palestine was to separate into two columns. The first column to make an assault heading north up the coastline. The second column was to parallel them more inland taking key points inland from the coast.

Coming north out of Palestine as well, the Free French were to make a direct march and assault on the City of Damascus.

Out of the east from TransJordan, the British led forces were to assault and control airbases in the northern part of Syria.

In the middle prong of the Allied invasion, the Free

French had a seemingly easier time then some of their compatriots. They were able to make a very rapid advance into the country and by June 12, 1941 were within ten miles of the city of Damascus.

To the left of the Free French forces the right column of the Australian division easily captured the city of Marjayun.

The far left column of the Australian division on June 9th came against some very heavy resistance at the hands of the Vichy forces.

The Australians gained the upper hand in the battle and were able to cross the Litany River on the coastal route. The path cleared and energy high to push on. Drive increasing with each success and troops pressed on.

From the island of Cyprus, 70 miles off the coast, a British commando unit affected a landing on the coast and aided the Australians in their success in crossing the river. Unfortunately, for the British commandos suffered heavy casualties from the landing and engagement. (67)

The aid was appreciated and necessary. Their losses not ignored. However, the battle and all troops had to maintain momentum or any gains thus far would be quickly lost.

Besides the Free French forces there was an additional three columns of British led troops heading for the city of Damascus.

The Allies knew the city was well defended and strongholds established in and around the city. This was going to be a challenge that needed careful planning.

When the British led troops approached the area around Kisswe, a strong point south of Damascus, the

Allied forces ready.

Troops were pushed around for several days by furious counter attacks. (68) An arduous back-and-forth tug-of-war. Neither side showing any sign surrender would come. The Vichy warned the German government that the British and Allied troops were ready for all sacrifice to themselves.

What were the Vichy and their Axis partners willing to do to continue? Were they ready for any sacrifice or crazy enough to not even consider that? Had the battlefield evened enough the only way a winner could be decided is...who wants it more?

# 15 VICHY COUNTER

The fast moving multipronged invasion of the Allied forces led by the British into Vichy French Syria left the Vichy military forces in the area in awe and scrambling for organization.

The initial blast at the start of the invasion was enough to send the Vichy forces reeling, but they quickly reorganized themselves and restructured their defenses ahead of the Allied forces. Their fast defense came unexpectedly to the invading British led troops.

The Vichy led forces then mounted a large counter attack near the area of Jebel Druze that effectively cut Allied communication between the cities of Deraa and Damascus.

This counter attack by the Vichy French cut the invasion force in two. One side unable to communicate with the other, divide and conquer strategy.

This was a well-scouted move by the Vichy military. This one counter attack significantly slowed the advancing military and crippled their once united front.

In the wake of the first successful counter attack, the Vichy forces quickly mounted another near the city of Kumcitra. The idea...to keep momentum of strikes rapid and unexpected. Giving the British no opportunity to scramble to their feet or recover between blows.

The counter attack unsuspected by the British resulted in the capturing of the greater part of the 1st Royal Fusiliers Battalion. The plan worked and this capture was the first evidence.

The loss of nearly an entire battalion was a large cost to

the Allies and one they could not afford to pay. Already very short on personnel and manpower the loss of this brigade was a huge hit to the invading Allied forces.

Gaining speed and momentum from these successful counter attacks the Vichy forces organized a third, hoping for the same impact to their enemies.

This new counter attack took place around the city of Marjayun. Easily and quickly recapturing the city from the Australian forces that had advanced earlier to another position.

This too could prove a dramatic assault with dire consequences to the Allied forces. In the wake of their rapid advancement, the Australians moving positions...that left the main road to the citywide open and undefended. (69)

The British, despite its loss of the much-needed battalion and ferocity of the counter attacks launched by the Vichy forces, they pressed on undaunted.

Although these attacks were unexpected, they were surprisingly easily blocked or repelled. Unfortunately, the attacks were successful in slowing down the still fast-paced British advances in the Vichy French territory. (70)

However, the Allied troops still had a few tricks left in their sleeve.

To the surprise of the Vichy military, the British had assigned two more columns of troops coming into Syria from the northeast. These two columns were paralleling each other about 100 miles apart.

The lower column was a mechanized unit. They were

ordered to proceed to the city of Palmyra. Once in the city, they were to secure the airfields and render them useless to not only Vichy aircraft by Axis aircraft as well.

Once the city was secure and the airfields disabled to enemy craft, the lower column was to proceed to the very important highway junction near the area of Homs.

The highway junction was important to control for military use. These highway systems were overland routes to resupply and reinforce their troops with resources and other scarce supplies.

Unfortunately, this would be a double edge sword. This also provided easier deployment of troops quickly, that was the benefit of both sides. The Allies needed to take these opportunities away from the Vichy military, maintaining access for themselves.

The lower column securing their two first objectives, were then to proceed to the oil pipeline from Tripoli. These British troops were to take control of the pipeline from the Vichy forces guarding it. (71)

To the Allies having control of the oil pipeline was imperative to their success. Their control of the pipeline would stop the flow of oil to the Vichy French military in the country rendering there war machines useless.

Now that only halts oil production. These troops still must control outbound stores and halt inbound reserves of enemy oil reserves without interfering with their own means of resupplying troops.

---

The upper column of British soldiers, led by British Major General Glubb, consisted of British led Arabs from TransJordan that originally stationed in Iraq. Major Glubb and his troops had the objective of heading to the city of Aleppo.

The Allies knew that Aleppo was of strategic importance to not only the Vichy military but to the Nazi regime as well.

Two weeks prior the Germans had begun a concentration of air power at Aleppo and its airfields. This gave the Germans the start to a forward airbase to conduct raids and missions on Allied positions in the region. An ability the Germans had not had before.

After Major Glubb and his men secured the city of Aleppo and its many numerous airfields, they had orders to proceed on to the city of Latakia.

Latakia was the northern most seaport in Syria. This port city was important to the British for two reasons. Control of the city and its ports could stop any influx of supplies, reinforcements, and military from entering the country to aid the Vichy military already engaged in battle.

Essentially, it would finish cutting the country off to the Vichy military.

The second reason Latakia was important to the British. It would be extremely vital to the defense of Cyprus that was only 70 miles off the coast of Syria. (72)

The island of Cyprus was important for the British to control. It gave a point in the Mediterranean that was used as a forward operating base for various missions and assaults around the Mediterranean area.

Cyprus provided large naval ports for repairs, refueling, and rearming. It also had large airfields able to hold, repair, and rearm multiple long range and short-range fighter planes. Cyprus also provided bases for ground troops as well, used throughout the Mediterranean world.

---

Things were looking slightly better for the British in the Middle East. By mid-June, General Wavell was able to make another brigade of troops from the 6th Division and the remnants of a mobile artillery unit.

After forming this new brigade, they were immediately placed at the disposal of General Wilson, who was heading the campaign in Syria. (73)

Even with heavy casualties on both sides of the engagement, the battle pressed on. This had been a numbers game all along, and was planned as best as possible with that in mind. Each side knowing any loss in momentum lost them tactically on the field. The cost greater with each tug back and forth for ultimate control.

A huge push by the 5th Indian Brigade commanded by British General Brigadier Lloyd, with assistance by Free French troops. The Allies were finally able to capture the city of Damascus on June 21, 1941. (74)

A huge success for Allied forces. Although things were not looking promising to the Vichy government any longer, that is both, in Syria and back in France.

By June 25th, the Vichy government was beginning to see that their tenure in Syria was almost over unless something happened, dramatic and in their favor.

A telegram sent from Paris by the Vichy government to the German Political Department in Berlin, adds insight to actions behind the scenes:

"...*the French government has requested information on whether, in the event of a French call for help through German military action in Syria, the German reply "might be combined with a declaration cleared for publication that, in contrast to England, Germany does not call in question French rights in Syria.""* (75)

Though they were knowingly losing to the English in Syria, the Vichy government was still hesitant to ask for more German military assistance to thwart the British offensive.

The Vichy were learning many things though out this exchange. Having to jump through hoops for allies unwilling to offer more aid than they deemed necessary or even beneficial to themselves. The truth and cost of all they have done or agreed to along the way becoming increasingly more evident.

The Vichy realizing, slowly, they were protecting a huge interest for many…but in the end…there was still to be only one true benefactor. In this case, they were the workhorses while Axis leaders and their people reaped the rewards.

Now was possibly a good point to step back, assess, reorganize, and most important…restructure their true goal. If that was ever truly defined.

The Vichy government had promised Germany help, aid, and use of French territories in the German quests. It was the Vichy governments fear they would lose the territory completely if the German military stepped in to help them further.

In the end, this could mean zero benefit for all they gave.

# 16 FINAL PUSH

Finally…there was some light at the end of the tunnel for the Allied troops in the Middle East. Most specifically the British.

They had successfully shut down the large Iraqi revolt. Now they were able to use some of these obligated troops to put even more pressure on the Vichy government in Syria.

Towards the end of June, General Wavell, was able to make use of the 10th Indian Division in Syria. This division under the command of Lieutenant General E.P. Quinan, was previously stationed in Iraq aiding the British in the Iraqi revolt.

Until receiving orders, they had not played a large role in the efforts in Syria. The 10th Indian Division received their orders to move into Syria and aid the Allies against the Vichy forces. At both Wavell's order and Quinan's command. (76)

---

In the west of Syria along the Damour River, the Vichy troops were stubbornly resisting the Allied advances. The Allies were also encountering stiff resistance along the southern slopes of Lebanon as well. (77)

The harsh resistance offered by the Vichy forces is going to quickly diminish, once unable to be adequately resupplied and moved.

The British were occupying most of the vital routes in and around the country at this point. The resistance will prove futile for the Vichy French quickly, against the overwhelming, suddenly overwhelming, reorganized, and boosted Allied military.

During the course of the Iraqi revolt, the British Middle East Command, under the direction of Prime Minister Winston Churchill, created what was known as a Habforce.

This new British unit was created to relieve and support the British troops around the Habbanyia airfield during the Iraqi revolt.

The Habforce consisted of Jewish Hagenah soldiers, Arab regular soldiers plus a host of other assorted random recruits and troops.

At the order of the Middle East Command, the Habforce was deployed into Syria. The Habforce faced a brutal fight in and around the city of Palmyra. Finally taking control of the city and its airfields from the Vichy troops. (78)

Victory for the Allies. Another devastating loss for the Axis Powers. Allied forces strengthening with each grasp forward to push them ahead.

On July 7, 1941, the 17th Australian Brigade was able to cross the Damour River in the direction of Homs.

The city of Homs was important to the British because of its extensive highway junctions in the city.

The British needed control of all overland highway systems in Syria. As previously stated, to stop all access to Axis troops but keep their own routes open.

Having the city of Homs was instrumental in that goal.

---

By July 8[th,] the 10th Indian Division had faced and endured heavy air attacks by Axis bombers and fighter planes.

Although these assaults paired with strong resistance from Vichy ground forces, the Allies still captured the cities of Raqqa and Kameschle.

These two cities were key points for the Euphrates Province. (79)

---

July 9, 1941 saw the 21st Australian Brigade take the town of Homs. Ahead of the movement of the 17th Australian Brigade still pushing up the coast.

This successful undertaking removed the main obstacle for the Allied advancement on Beirut from the south, and increased the British control of now the majority of the highway infrastructure, and extending reach throughout the country. (80)

The Vichy French forces were feeling the effect of the Allied stranglehold on the country. The Vichy French battle lines and forces were beginning to thin out and run low on supplies and munitions.

The Vichy aware this fight could soon end if something very big did not occur for them to keep furiously fighting.

Much more was to come on July 9[th,]. The area in and beyond the city of Homs threatened more.

With the Australian 17th and 21st Brigades nearing, the

British 4th Calvary had already successfully cut the railways heading south. This made the railways unusable to the Vichy forces. While still allowing movement of Allied troops arriving. (81)

For the British and Allies more soldiers for the fight joined quickly.

Along the way, squadrons of Mounted English Yeomanry cleaned up behind the Damascus and Beirut drives routing out any leftover pockets of resistance.

An interesting note, Syria was the first time that the mounted cavalry had been used in this war. (82)

The city of Beirut…the last stronghold of the Vichy forces…now threatened from several directions.

Leading the threat against Beirut was the 16th Indian Brigade who had devastated enemy strongholds along the road near the city of Dimas. (83)

Truth and reality now staring them in the face the Vichy government and their forces knew that any further resistance was illogical.

The fact of total loss of control of the Northern Desert and the Euphrates Province. The threat of the inevitable loss of Beirut. It was now time…the game…was over. General Dentz of the Vichy forces had no other option but to ask for an armistice. (84)

# 17 ARMISTICE

The British government had made the decision to replace General Wavell in the Middle East Command. Wavell had been reassigned to the North Africa; his replacement was British General Auchinleck.

This decision came at the orders of Prime Minister Churchill.

He and General Wavell had a tumultuous relationship to start. The Prime Minister was unhappy with events as of late for the Middle Eastern forces. Not only the recent revolts in Iraq, the North African campaigns, the campaign on Cyprus, and the brief struggles in Syria.

To Churchill, all 'fires' contained for now allowed for the perfect opportunity for the shift in command.

At 6pm on July 11th General Auchinleck, as the Commander in Chief of Middle East Forces, received a message from General Dentz of the Vichy forces proposing to end the hostilities six hours later at midnight. (85)

General Dentz declared that he was ready to engage in talks with the British and allied commanders. He offered open dialog on the basis of a memorandum presented to him by the United States Consul in Beirut, presented him on behalf of the British Government.

General Dentz, then made it clear to the British that he could only have dialog with the British. (86)

Under orders from the Vichy government, Dentz could only deal with British representatives, and not the

Free French. The reason…to the Vichy government, the Free French were traitors and enemies of the state. Therefore negotiating with them could not take place.

The proposal, presented by General Dentz was considered by the Middle East War Council. All points weighed and understood.

The council also took into account the opinion of the United States Consul in Beirut who opened the dialog with General Dentz for the Allied forces.

The United States Consul later offered the Middle East War Council their decision. They believed General Dentz was completely insincere and speculated he was 'playing for time' in hopes of a German military rescue effort.

With the information at hand and the opinion of the United States Consul in Beirut, the Allies rejected General Dentz's proposal. Instead, the British presented the Vichy French, more importantly General Dentz with a proposal of their own.

The Middle East War Council called on Dentz to send his commanding officers to the British outpost on Haifa road. They informed General Dentz that his commanders needed to be there at or before 9am on July 12th.

If they were late or failed to show up the Allies informed Dentz the hostilities would continue relentlessly. (87) Dentz had no choice but to comply. However, before he did, he forwarded the information to the Vichy government back in France.

The Vichy government taken back by the strongly worded proposal of the British turned to the German government for council. The Vichy government asked the Nazi regime as to what they should do with the British proposal.

In a memo from the German Political Department, their answer was as this:

*" The French government has recently informed us that, through the American Consul General in Beirut, the English had sent to General Dentz proposals for the suspension of hostilities…" "…we had thereupon replied to the French Government that we were convinced of the insincerity of the English intentions and could therefore only warn the French against making agreements with the English."* (88)

In hindsight, it seems ironic that the two governments who had no real military investments in the campaign were the voice of reason to their respective allies.

The United States informs the Allies and the Middle East War Council of the insincerity of the Vichy French. On the other side, the Germans are informing the Vichy government to the true intentions of the British.

Neither the United States nor the Germans had any militaristic investments in the campaign through Syria. The difference between the pair…the U.S. backed up offers made. However, it is curious that the Vichy left to fight alone, and doubt intent of their German allies at the end of days in Syria. Why would Vichy consider their advice now?

If the Vichy refrained from asking for further aid during the fight…why would they seek their answers later?

Regardless to the German response, the Vichy government Vichy representatives arrived at the British Haifa road outpost and with time to spare before the 9am deadline. Then was swiftly taken by the Allies, to Acre in Palestine, to begin negotiations. (89)

Rather than attend the negotiations himself General Dentz sent his second in command General de Vedillac in his place.

This is where many...or at least two of the 'Main Players' meet for the conclusion.

It was known that de Vedillac was more pro-British and less anti-de Gaulle then Dentz.(90)The discussions in Acre were definitely one sided.

The Allies were represented by General Sir Henry Wilson, Air Commodore L.O. Brown, Captain J.A.V. Morse of the Royal Navy, and General Catroux of the Free French (who had already been condemned to death by the Vichy government).

The Vichy government was represented solely by General de Vedillac. Leaving this meeting de Vedillac versus the Allied Forces. (91)

Now I am sure the Vichy are reconsidering, more now than before, all they gave...with no benefit. However, the biggest slap to the Vichy face is yet to come.

The terms of the armistice presented were considered generous and non-humiliating by all sides. The British were giving the Vichy French a little wiggle room as far as what they had to give up.

Good faith on their part, though the Vichy still had yet to earn that. One of the first terms of the armistice was Allies were to occupy Syria and Lebanon for the duration of the war. The Allies would also take over all war materials, public utilities, communications, arsenals, harbors, and airfields throughout Syria and Lebanon.

An added stipulation...all prisoners of war held were to be released, from both sides. Rather fair all around.

However, upon release these Vichy P.O.W.'s were given three choices they could either make reparations, join the Free French or stay in Syria as non-combatants. (92)

There was no stipulation set or requested of Allied P.O.W.' released by the Vichy.

The Vichy forces suffered nearly 9,000 casualties while the Allies took around 1,500 casualties. (93)

---

At the end of the battles on the field. All agreements signed and sealed. This single, nearly forgotten, or possibly hidden campaign only lasted thirty-three days as part of that much larger world war lasting years more.

The importance then was simply territory. Control.

Unfortunately, the landscape in the Middle East has not entirely changed. The only difference is the earned the autonomy promised…and that power then transferred to others, yet the battles for territory and control remained.

There are different players in the game now and any involvement of other political powers in the world take place on a different field or behind closed doors.

For 'Operation Exporter', many issues and challenges had been faced and overcome. The final tolls not yet tabulated, per our discussion.

However, forces and personnel lost was significant in comparison to other battles with in the world at war.

Allied forces, short on manpower at the start, still faced 1,500 causalities that I am aware.

For the Vichy…their battle in Syria over…but much more was to come for the government entity. This battle cost them greatly and those who had offered them aid with a staggering 9,000 causalities.

# 18 INSULT TO INJURY

The armistice between Great Britain and the Vichy government became known as the Acre Pact, since it was negotiated and signed in the city of Acre in Palestine.

Late in the evening about 10pm on July 12, 1941, the Acre Pact is initialed and final draft approved by all the representatives of the Allies and the one representative of the Vichy government.

Two days later, the Acre Pact was official on July 14, 1941 being signed by both General Wilson on behalf of the British and, General de Vedillac for the Vichy government. (94) The other Allied representatives signed the pact after these two, there was no other Vichy signatures to obtain.

The Acre Pact officially ended the five-week Syrian campaign of World War 2. This pact was the first such pact between Great Britain and France since the age of Napoleon.

An important document with much historical significance. Bore from a battle nearly forgotten with time.

There would be several more skirmishes between these two great nations during the first couple of years of World War 2 on land, sea, and air. Nothing quite the same as events in Syria.

Now, the story takes another interesting and curious turn.

General de Vedillac had gone to Acre to negotiate the terms of the armistice, on behalf of General Dentz, at the request of the Vichy French government first initialed the agreement on July 12th, and General de Vedillac signed the terms officially on July 14, 1941.

This we know and have proof of. However, strange and unexplainable 'things' began occurring during this process.

As de Vedillac was preparing to sign the pact in Acre, the lights in the building blacked out rendering the building completely dark.

In response to the black out the Allied commanders had a message dispatcher bring his motorcycle into the room to be able to use the headlight of the motorcycle to finish signing the agreement.

The battle that started in the early morning hours of June 8th was officially ended by headlight of an Allied dispatcher's motorcycle. (95)

By now most figured this Vichy government...is nearly done.

However, life has quite the sense of humor...ask those you fight blindly and arrogantly until you have nothing left...not even supporters.

Some of the following events or...coincidences...may have been planned. Depends on which theorist you ask.

Just as some believe this was such an entirely botched operation by many powerful men...it was hidden from history.

Or...was because some used their personal feelings to lead when a business mind was needed?

Again...you decide.

I just found an interesting story to tell. Political sides or allegiances mean nothing here…just facts of a period of 33 days in our world's history I never knew about before and thought I would share.

To add another insult to the Vichy French government the Pact officially signed on Bastille Day 1941. Bastille Day to the French is their celebration of independence. Signing on Bastille Day was a demoralizing blow to the Vichy French government and the population of France.

To the French people that prior year they watched as the government sign over Paris and large chunks of France to the invading Nazi regime, now they are witnessing their Vichy government sign over Syria and Lebanon to the conquering British.

Another insult to the Vichy government and supports came when, the Free French forces, was heavily represented in not only the talks of the armistice agreement but in the signing of the end of the conflict as well. (96)

Of course, these events happened concurrently, and amounted to just a really bad day. However, individually analyzed each component is rather amusing.

Upon completion of the armistice agreement between the Allies and Vichy France, Great Britain immediately moved to incorporate Syria and Lebanon into what is known as the Sterling Bloc.

The Sterling Bloc was a legal procedure, it was groups of countries, or territories that based the value of their currency to the British pound sterling or these countries used the pound as their own currency.

This move by the English and the economic influence of the Middle East Supply Center in Cairo convinced the Free French that Great Britain opposed any type of French power in Syria and Lebanon.

This action, its implications, and questions of the Free French government led to several disputes and arguments between these two allies during the remaining years of the war. (97)

Churchill expressed restoring France to its former glory. These are the ideals the Free French used when taking their government back. However, even allies get limits.

According to the agreements of the Acre Pact, Article 21 allowed the setup of a Commission of Control.

The objective of this commission was to supervise the execution of this pact. Their first meeting on July 16, 1941 at Ain Sofar in Lebanon under the direction and supervision of Major General J.I. Chrystall.(98)

---

Releasing P.O.W.'s, as prescribed by the Acre Pact, by September 27, 1941 all Vichy French that did not want to join the ranks of the Free French or want to stay in Syria as non-combatants were removed from the area. All part of the three options offered to Vichy troops as per the armistice discussion. Under supervision of the commission, these Vichy French were transported back to Vichy held southern France. (99)

Mandated by the pact as well, the Vichy French had to return the Allied prisoners of war under their control.

Some of these British and Allied prisoners had been removed from Syria by the Vichy government at some point. This placed the loyal Vichy troops in an unfortunate position since this breeched the pact.

The most shocking detail the British learned was that many of these prisoners were removed by the Vichy government AFTER the Acre Pact had been initialed. (100)

This blatant act would generally breech or nullify an agreement or contract. This grand scale action needed to be swift to mitigate damages either way.

Learning of the actions by the Vichy French after the armistice was in place, the British and Allies reacted immediately.

Since there was, a delay on the part of the Vichy government returning British and Allied prisoners agreed to in the armistice, the British arrested and detained General Dentz, plus twenty-nine of his most senior officers.

The British sent their new prisoners to a detention center in Palestine. As the Vichy government slowly returned British and Allied prisoners under their control, the British slowly released the Vichy general and his staff from the detention center in Palestine. (101)

The Free French government wanted to maintain the Vichy French troops in Syria and Lebanon as long as possible.

They had their own agenda here. Their own theories. The Free French had hopes that a prolonged period of exposure of propaganda to the Vichy forces would help to obtain new recruits from within the Vichy ranks. Not a new tactic in a war by any military.

The British and Allies had other ideas. They simply

wanted the Vichy troops out of the area as quickly as possible.(102) No more games with or for the Vichy.

The British did not want the threat of an uprising or attempted coup to take their focus from other goings on in the war. This matter was dealt with and simply needed enforcement. There were more pressing issues in this world, at that time that needed their full attention.

The Free French desires were a little over eager and optimistic. Although, all fell into place when it needed to.

It is easy to understand their theory and wish to utilize propaganda tactics considering the sheer number of prisoners alone. If there were, any possibility that would work...the addition to military personnel would have been incredible at that time.

From the 37,736 Vichy troops stationed in the area only 5,668 declared to be in favor and loyal to the Free French cause. (103)

# 19 IMPACTS

The campaign into Syria and Lebanon had implications on all those involved, directly or indirectly. These results will have an effect during the course of the remainder of the war.

With his initiative in the Syria campaign and his cooperation with British and Allied troops, Free French leader General Charles de Gaulle became the prominent figure and symbol for the French resistance to the German aggression. (104)

Under his direction and leadership, he was able to organize the French resistance movement through France to wreak havoc on the German military complex in the country.

He quickly became enemy number one for not only the Axis Powers but also for his own countries government of Vichy France, the recognized government.

After the conclusion of the campaign into Syria and Lebanon, General de Gaulle recognized the vital need for unity in command. He was witness to the benefits and the power of unity.

He recommended this for not only his command of the Free French forces but for the whole of the Allies. With his big picture realization, General de Gaulle placed all Free French forces throughout the Middle East under the British Commander in Chief for operational purposes. (105)

British General Sir Henry Wilson, who was in charge of executing the Syrian campaign and armistice agreements, appointed Free French General Catroux High Commissioner of the France Libre in Syria and Lebanon.

In accordance with this appointment, the Free French took over all civil administration in Syria and Lebanon under the direction of General Catroux. (106)

Catroux faced struggle immediately as the new High Commissioner. With the dissolution of the Vichy governments in Syria and Lebanon that left a void due to the lack of men with administrative abilities. This void severely felt by not only General Catroux, but the local populations as well. There were constant complaints and reports from the Syrian and Lebanese citizens about the former Vichy officials who stayed in the region as non-combatants.

These former Vichy officials that retained their former positions. Most of the claims stated they were corrupt and discredited to the people.(107)

With these individuals remaining in the area, will the issues ever be laid to rest?

Germany refused to leave things alone in the Middle East and weighed in on the matter when provided opportunity. The Foreign Minister in Berlin sent a memo out to his personnel expressing his thoughts:

> *"...Regard for the French rule in Syria has far imposed on us a certain reserve in supporting demands of the Arabs for political freedom and independence. With the collapse of French resistance against England in Syria, the reason for this reserve has been eliminated..."*

> *"...This propaganda must be carried out under the slogan "The Axis fights for the freedom of the Arabs"; appropriate Italian cooperation is to be arranged."* (108)

Had the British not acted in Syria when they did or if

the campaign in Syria had not been in British favor the outcome of World War 2 could and most likely would have gone dramatically different.

The Vichy French government had really left Britain and the Allies no other choice but to occupy the mandated territories of Syria and Lebanon.

They needed this territory, and knew they would not receive what was originally promised.

It was very well established that the Vichy government was weak and willing to appease the Nazi Germany government at every turn in the war. Even if required to be deceptive. They were not to be trusted.

# CONCLUSION

Let us just recap what we know. You choose sides if you like…create your own theories or realizations…I will simply report the facts for others to debate, if they choose.

The Vichy government was willing to aid and supply the Iraqi militants, revolting against British rule, by way of Syria. They were also allowing the Axis Powers to aid the Iraqi rebels through the mandated territories as well.

The Vichy government had given the Axis Powers the opportunity to use the airfields inside Syria and Lebanon as a forwarding base to attack British and Allied positions throughout the Middle East area. The British knew no other option was available but to rid the Vichy threat entirely in the Middle East before it escalated once again

.

The British and Allies knew that they could not allow the Germans or Axis Powers to become established permanently in the Middle East. Peaceful coexistence and use of the area would never be equitable or possible.

With the British being spread so thin throughout their vast but vanishing empire they would not have the resources and manpower to deal with them.

Without this 'hub' in the Middle East, the British would have lost their much needed oil supply from Iraq. The British global empire would have been cut in half, communications would have been severed, and most important the British and Allies would have lost access and control of the Suez Canal.

Now, looking at the reverse facts. The 'what if's' in this battle. Just to have a broader view.

German and Axis Power establishment in the Middle East would give them the valuable oil reserves and resources in the area. They would then get control of the Suez Canal and the Mediterranean Sea.

The Germans would be able to completely encircle Turkey and have complete access to the Straights of Darnell and Black Sea. The Straights of Darnell and Black Sea would have given the Germans another front to launch their invasion into Russia.

Which leads us to a Pandora's box of issues beyond this 33-day fight.

Now…given this information…what should have happened? What was best or needed to happen?

Those questions have many answers. Just as any possible outcome, other than the events that occurred, would have changed probably more than we realize. That is during the war and possibly affecting even the world's landscape today.

That…we will never know.

What is so interesting about fact is, it is unchanging if held, presented, and treated as truth.

Unfortunately, as we have seen here, fact can also be a matter of perception or perspective.

In truth, the facts meant something else to each 'player' involved. Each 'truth' was different and seemed to be based on the most beneficial to the beholder.

Given the facts, and knowing the players involved in this particular engagement. I can see and even understand why there would, could and is theories or 'conspiracies' surrounding this battle.

It is not hard to see why the Allies would not want to discuss Operation Exporter much in the open.

Anymore, no matter the facts presented on any topic someone seems to wiggle some conspiracy into it.

I thought this was an interesting story, with information to back it up. It was and is something that is not discussed or mentioned a lot. After doing my research I wanted to present the facts as I found them and let, you the reader decide the rest.

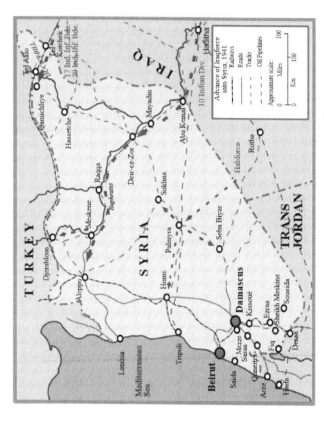

By Stephen Kirrage, CC BY 3.0, https://commons.wikimedia.org/w/index.php?curid=14109207

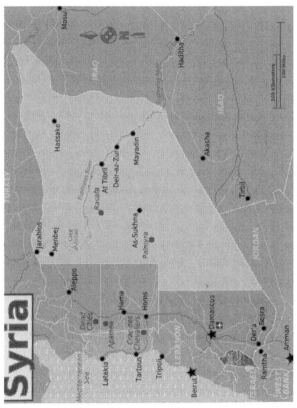

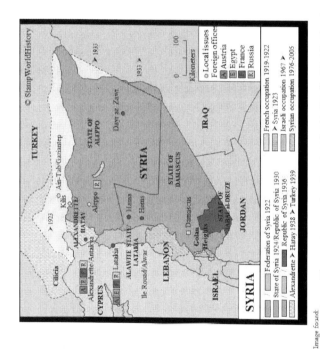

Image found:
http://www.stampworldhistory.com/country-profiles-2/asia/syria°/.D8°/.B3°/.D9°/.8.3°/.D8°/.B1°/.D9°/.8A°/.D8°/.

# END NOTES

1. Article 22; League of Nations
2. Ochsenwald, W. and Fisher, S. ;The Middle East a History; pg. 470
3. Ibid. pg. 470
4. Franco-Turkish Mutual Aid Agreement
5. Oschsenwald, W. and Fisher, S. ; The Middle East a History; pg. 470
6. Ibid. pg. 470
7. Ibid. pg. 470
8. General Archibald Wavell
9. General Sir Archibald Wavell
10. Wilson, Henry Maitland, Wilson, Baron, b. 1881
11. Charles de Gaulle biography
12. General Catroux
13. Oschsenwald, W. and Fisher, S. ; The Middle East a History; pg. 470
14. Weizsacker; The State Secretary to the Embassy in Turkey
15. The State Secretary to the Embassy in Italy
16. El Husseini, Mohammed Amin, The Grand Mufti to Adolf Hitler
17. Papen; The Ambassador in Turkey to the Foreign Ministry
18. Oschsenwald, W. and Fisher, S. ; The Middle East a History; pg. 470
19. Ibid. pg. 470
20. Black, C.E. ; Vichy Puppet Show; pg. 57
21. Time Magazine; World War: Middle Eastern Theater: The Syrian Show Begins
22. Wavell, A. ; Operations in the Middle East 7Feb1941-15Jul1941
23. White, W. ; Britain's Conquest of Syria; pg. 30
24. Kroll; The Charge d' Affaires in Turkey to the Foreign Ministry
25. Woermann; Memorandum by the Director of the

Political Department

26. Schmidt; Memorandum by an Official of the Foreign Minister's Secretariat

27. Abetz; The Embassy in Paris to the Foreign Ministry

28. Darlan, F. ; Protocols Signed at Paris on May 27 and May 28, 1941

29. Black; pg. 57

30. Ibid; pg. 58

31. Wavell, A. ; <u>Operations in the Middle East 7Feb1941-15Jul1941</u>

32. Black ; pg. 58

33. Churchill, W. ; <u>The Second World War, Volume III, The Grand Alliance</u>; pg. 226

34. Wavell, A. ; <u>Operations in the Middle East 7Feb1941-15Jul1941</u>

35. Ibid.

36. Ibid.

37. Ibid.

38. Ibid.

39. Ibid.

40. Ibid.

41. Ibid.

42. Ibid.

43. Ibid.

44. Churchill; pg. 228

45. Eisenhower, D. ; pg.23

46. Wilbur, W. ; pg. 31

47. Ibid.

48. Hull, C. ; <u>Statements on Franco-German Collaboration</u>

49. Wavell, A. ; <u>Operations in the Middle East 7Feb1941-15Jul1941</u>

50. Black ; pg. 59

51. Time Magazine; <u>World War: Middle Eastern Theater: Mixed Show</u>

52. Time Magazine; <u>World War: Middle Eastern</u>

Theater: Mixed Show
53. Ibid.
54. Ibid.
55. Hull; Secretary of State Hull's Statement on Franco-German Collaboration June 13, 1941
56. Time Magazine; World War: Middle Eastern Theater: The Syrian Show Begins
57. Time Magazine; World War: Middle Eastern Theater: Mixed Show
58. Churchill, W. ; Debate in the House of Commons, June 10, 1941
59. Hull, C. ; Secretary of State Hull's Statement on Franco-German Collaboration June 13, 1941
60. Time Magazine; World War: Middle Eastern Theater: Mixed Show
61. Ibid.
62. Ibid.
63. Ibid.
64. Abetz; The Embassy in Paris to the Foreign Ministry
65. Time Magazine; World War: Middle Eastern Theater: Mixed Show
66. Ibid.
67. Wavell, A. ; Operations in the Middle East 7Feb1941-15Jul1941
68. Time Magazine; World War: Middle Eastern Theater: Mixed Show
69. Wavell, A. ; Operations in the Middle East 7Feb1941-15Jul1941
70. Ibid.
71. Time Magazine; World War: Middle Eastern Theater: Mixed Show
72. Ibid.
73. Wavell, A. ; Operations in the Middle East 7Feb1941-15Jul1941
74. Ibid.
75. Woermann; Memorandum by an Official of the

Foreign Minister's Secretariat

76. Wavell, A. and Auchinleck, C.; <u>Operations in the Middle East 5Jul1941-31Oct1941</u>
77. Auchinleck, C. ; <u>Operations in the Middle East 5Jul1941-31Oct1941</u>
78. Wavell, A. ; <u>Operations in the Middle East 7Feb1941-15Jul1941</u>
79. Auchinleck, C. ; <u>Operations in the Middle East 5Jul1941-31Oct1941</u>
80. Ibid.
81. Ibid.
82. Time Magazine; <u>World War: Middle Eastern Theater: Mixed Show</u>
83. Auchinleck, C.; <u>Operations in the Middle East 5Jul1941-31Oct1941</u>
84. Ibid.
85. Ibid.
86. Ibid.
87. Ibid.
88. Woermann; The Director of the Political Department to the Embassy in Italy and to the Embassy in Paris
89. Auchinleck, C.; <u>Operations in the Middle East 5Jul1941-31Oct1941</u>
90. Time Magazine; <u>World War: Acre Pact</u>
91. Auchinleck, C.; <u>Operations in the Middle East 5Jul1941-31Oct1941</u>
92. Time Magazine; <u>World War: Mediterranean Theater: Exit With a Flourish</u>
93. Ibid.
94. Auchinleck, C.; <u>Operations in the Middle East 5Jul1941-31Oct1941</u>
95. Time Magazine; <u>World War: Acre Pact</u>
96. Ibid.
97. Ocshenwald, W. and Fisher, S. ; The Middle East a History; pg. 470
98. Auchinleck, C.; <u>Operations in the Middle East</u>

5Jul1941-31Oct1941
99. Ibid.
100.Ibid.
101.Ibid.
102.Ibid.
103.Ibid.
104.Black; Vichy Puppet Show; pg. 61
105.Auchinleck, C.; Operations in the Middle East
5Jul1941-31Oct1941
106.Ibid.
107.Ibid.
108.Ribbentrop; The Foreign Minister to the Foreign
Minister's Secretariat

# BIBLIOGRAPHY

Auchinleck, General Sir Claude J.E. "Commander in Chief of Middle East Force"; Operations in the Middle East 5Jul1941-31Oct1941; submitted to the Secretary of War March 8, 1942: reprinted Tuesday August 20, 1946 *The London Gazette*: accessed on April 20, 2010 at : http://www.LondonGazette.com/archives

Black, C.E. (Department of History, Princeton University); Vichy's Puppet Show: *Current History Volume 1 Sept-Feb 1941-1942*; p. 57-62

Churchill, Winston; Debate in the House of Commons June 10, 1941; accessed on April 21, 2010; http://www.ibiblio.org/pha/policy/1941/41606k.html

Churchill, Winston; The Second World War, Volume III, The Grand Alliance; Houghton Mifflin Co., Boston, Mass; p. 224-237: accessed April 21, 2010. http://mtholyoke.edu/acad/intrel/Petroleum/iraq.html

Hull, Cordell; Secretary of State Hull's Statement on Franco-German Collaboration June 13, 1941; accessed on April 21, 2010; http://www.ibiblio.org/pha/policy/1941/41613a.html

Ochsenwald, William and Fisher, Sydney Nettleton; The Middle East a History; 7th edition, McGraw Hill, New York, NY: 2011; p.470-471

Time Magazine; World War: Middle Eastern Theater: Mixed Show; Monday June 23, 1941: accessed April 20, 2010; http://www.time.com/time/magazine/article/9,9171,

851152,00.html

Time Magazine; World War: Acre Pact; Monday July 21, 1941: accessed on April 20, 2010; http://www.time.com/time/magazine/article/0,9171, 765788,00.html

Time Magazine; World War: Mediterranean Theater: Exit with a Flourish; Monday July 28, 1941; accessed on April 13, 2010; http://www.time.com/time/magazine/article/0,9171, 795404,00.html

Time Magazine; World War: Middle Easter Theater: The Syrian Show Begins; Monday June 16, 1941: accessed on April 13, 2010; http://www.time.com/time/magazine/article/0,9171, 765709,00.html

Wavell, General Sir Archibald P. "Commander in Chief Middle East Force"; Operations in the Middle East 7Feb1941-15Jul1941; submitted to the Secretary of War September 5, 1941: reprinted Tuesday July 2, 1946 *The London Gazette*: accessed on April 20, 2010; http://LondonGazette.com/archives

White, Wilbur; Britain's Conquest of Syria; *Current History Volume I Sept-Feb 1941-1942:* p. 30-31

Weizsacker; *The State Secretary to the Embassy in Turkey (telegram)*: January 8, 1941, No. 15 [Documents on German Foreign Policy 1918-1945; Series D, Volume III: The War Years 1940-1941: United States Government Printing Office, 1960: Publication 7083, Washington D.C.] p.1053

Weizsacker; *The State Secretary to the Embassy in Turkey (telegram)*: September 12, 1940, No. 1253: [Documents on German Foreign Policy 1918-1945; Series D,

Volume III: The War Years 1940-1941: United States Government Printing Office, 1960: Publication 7083, Washington D.C.] p. 65

El Husseini, Mohammed Amin; *The Grand Mufti to Adolf Hitler.* January 20, 1941, No. 680[Documents on German Foreign Policy 1918-1945; Series D, Volume III: The War Years 1940-1941; United States Government Printing Office, 1960: Publication 7083, Washington D.C.] p. 1281

Papen; *The Ambassador in Turkey to the Foreign Ministry*: January 28, 1941: No.722 [Documents on German Foreign Policy 1918-1945; Series D, Volume III: The War Years 1940-1941: United States Government Printing Office, 1960: Publication 7083, Washington D.C.] p. 1344

Kroll; *The Charge d'Affaires in Turkey to the Foreign Ministry*; May 2, 1941: No. 432 [Documents on German Foreign Policy 118-1945; Series D, Volume XII: The War Years 1941: United States Government Printing Office, 1962: Publication 7384; Washington D.C.] p. 686

Woermann; *Memorandum by the Director of the Political Department*; May 9, 1941: No. 479 [Document on German Foreign Policy 1918-1945; Series D, Volume XII: The War Years 1941: United States Government Printing Office, 1962: Publication 7382; Washington D.C.] p.744

Schmidt; *Memorandum by an Official of the Foreign Minister's Secretariat*; May 11, 1941: No. 491 [Document on German Foreign Policy 1918-1945; Series D, Volume XII: The War Years 1941: United States Government Printing Office, 1962: Publication 7382; Washington D.C.] p. 764

Abetz; *The Embassy in Paris to the Foreign Minister*; May 24, 1941: No.546 [Document on German Foreign Policy 1918-1945; Series D, Volume XII: The War Years 1941: United States Government Printing Office, 1962: Publication 7382; Washington D.C.] p. 867

Darlan; *Protocols Signed at Paris on May 27 and May 8, 1941*; May 28, 1941: No.559 [

Document on German Foreign Policy 1918-1945; Series D, Volume XII: The War Years 1941: United States Government Printing Office, 1962: Publication 7382; Washington D.C.] p. 892

Abetz; *The Embassy in Paris to the Foreign Ministry*; June 11, 1941: No.616 [Document on German Foreign Policy 1918-1945; Series D, Volume XII: The War Years 1941: United States Government Printing Office, 1962: Publication 7382; Washington D.C.] p.1008

Woermann; *Memorandum by the Director of the Political Department*; June 25, 1941: No.19 [Documents on German Foreign Policy 1918-1945; Series D; Volume XIII: The War Years 1941: United States Printing Office; 1964, Publication 7682; Washington D.C.] p. 22

Woermann; *The Director of the Political Department to the Embassy in Italy and to the Embassy in Paris*; July 12, 1941: No.101 [Documents on German Foreign Policy 1918-1945; Series D; Volume XIII: The War Years 1941: United States Printing Office; 1964, Publication 7682; Washington D.C.] p. 128

Ribbentrop; *The Foreign Minister to the Foreign Minister's Secretariat*; July 20, 1941: No.132 [Documents on German Foreign Policy 1918-1945; Series D; Volume XIII: The War Years 1941: United States Printing

Office; 1964, Publication 7682; Washington D.C.] p. 188

Article 22; Of the League of Nations www.mideastweb.org/leaguemand.htm; accessed on March 22, 2018

Franco-Turkish Mutual Aid Agreement; June 1939; http://indiana.edu/~league/1939.htm; accesses on March 22, 2018

General Archibald Wavell; https://www.historylearningsite.co.uk/world-war-two/military-commanders-of-world-war-two/general-archibald-wavell/; accessed on March 24, 2018

General Sir Archibald Wavell 1883-1950; https://www.historyof war.org/articles/people_wavell.html; accessed on March 24, 2018

Wilson, Henry Maitland Wilson, Baron, b.1881; https://catalog.archives.gov/id/10572454; accessed on March 24, 2018

Charles de Gaulle biography; https://www.biographies.net/politicians/Charles_de_Gaulle.net; accessed on March 25, 2018

Gencral Catroux; https://www.chemindemoire.gouv.fre/catroux.net; accessed on March 24, 2018

Eisenhower, Dwight D.; Crusade in Europe; DoubleDay & Company Inc; 1948; The Country Life Press; Garden City, N.Y.

# ABOUT THE AUTHOR

I have always had a love of history. My family growing up was always discussing family history or world history. So ever since I was a little kid history has always fascinated me.

I have always remembered the phrase "More knowledge has been lost over the ages then what is remembered". To me, I find that to be so true and I like to learn what we have forgotten. To know and to be able to tell people about historical events or people is a passion of mine.

Indiana Jones was my childhood hero, he thirst for adventure and knowledge was what I wanted to do. He had a knack for bringing history and stories alive, and that's what I have always wanted to do, just without the Hollywood affects.

I have a teenage son, who challenges me everyday and he is starting to get the history bug as well. My wife is my guiding light and my voice of reason, she keeps me wrangled in to reality.

I write history differently than most. I write it like I talk about it, I try to be engaging with the audience, giving them points of thought or questions to ask themselves. It is a unique way to write history, but I believe it personalizes every story for every reader.

I hope that I will be able to tell many more historical stories to the present or even the future.

J P Hyde

Made in the USA
Las Vegas, NV
08 January 2022

40756319R00068